Commendations for *Who Is the Holy Spirit?*

"Malcolm Yarnell is perhaps the greatest living Baptist theologian, and *Who Is the Holy Spirit?* is among the best of his writings. In this substantive and accessible book, we are given a biblically faithful portrayal of the Holy Spirit and are reminded of the Spirit's intimate involvement in our lives. Highly recommended for college and seminary students, pastors, and professors."

—*Bruce Ashford, provost and dean of faculty, Southeastern Baptist Theological Seminary*

"Beautifully written and thoughtfully presented, Malcolm Yarnell has given us a readable and accessible introduction to the theology of the Holy Spirit. Orthodox and evangelical in its convictions, *Who Is the Holy Spirit?* provides us with a clear and theologically-shaped interpretation of both Old and New Testament pictures of the third person of the Holy Trinity. Pastoral in its tone with an application focus throughout, this small volume exceeds expectations with its insightful depth, careful biblical exegesis, and its engaging use of the best of Christian tradition. It is a genuine joy to recommend this fine volume to new believers, church leaders, students, and pastors alike."

—*David S. Dockery, president, Trinity International University*

"I have been learning pneumatology from Malcolm Yarnell since the days I was his PhD student. His method as a systematic theologian who prioritizes biblical exegesis with pastoral motivation makes his books vital and valuable. This book is no exception. I am grateful to see its publication so many more can have the blessings and benefits of learning from Malcolm Yarnell that I and many students have had."

—*Jason G. Duesing, provost, associate professor of historical theology, Midwestern Baptist Theological Seminary*

"This is a book about the Holy Spirit, but it is also a book about worship. In reading these pages you will not simply have your mind sharpened, you will also have your heart formed as you consider God the Holy Spirit. I am confident this book will stir your affections for the gospel, the triune God, and specifically the Holy Spirit, the giver of life, who is worthy of adoration and praise."

—*J.T. English, pastor of training, The Village Church Institute, The Village Church, Flower Mound, TX*

"Malcolm Yarnell has never been afraid to tackle difficult or seemingly neglected theological topics, and this book is no different. He gives us a perfect balance between scholarship and practicality. *Who Is the Holy Spirit?* exquisitely surveys the Scripture leaving no doubt who the Holy Spirit is and what He does."

—*Mark David Forrest, senior pastor, Lakeside Baptist Church, Granbury, TX*

"Here is a fresh and faithful restatement of the biblical doctrine of the Holy Spirit from one of our finest Baptist theologians. Deep soundings in both the Old and New Testaments reveal the splendor of the Spirit's person and the efficacy of his divine work. *Who Is the Holy Spirit?* is a book to build up the people of God!"

—*Timothy George, founding dean, professor of divinity, Beeson Divinity School*

"Malcolm Yarnell is one of the outstanding voices in Baptist scholarship today, both a careful thinker and a faithful teacher. These gifts are in full evidence in this new book. *Who Is the Holy Spirit?* is richly biblical and thoughtful, and yet concise —a very rare achievement."

—*R. Albert Mohler Jr., president, The Southern Baptist Theological Seminary*

"Many often accidentally refer to the Holy Spirit with the pronoun 'It' rather than 'He' or 'Him.' Almost no one does so with the Father or the Son. Why? The Holy Spirit seems to many Christians to be almost an impersonal force. That's why we need this study by respected theologian Malcolm Yarnell. Yarnell excellently guides us through the Bible's revelation not just about what the Spirit does, but who He is. This book can help Christians relate personally to the Spirit of our God."

—*Russell D. Moore, president, The Ethics & Religious Liberty Commission of the Southern Baptist Convention*

"Malcolm Yarnell has written a much-needed work on the person and deity of the Holy Spirit. His excellent exegetical work through both the Old and New Testament is informative and clear. I am often asked by young pastors for a book list they could read, and this book is now in the top five of the list I give them."

—*Chris Osborne, senior pastor, Central Baptist Church, College Station, TX*

"Malcolm Yarnell does what few authors can – contemplate serious biblical theology while connecting with the heart and propelling the reader to action. This combination alone is worth the price of the book. His probing of the most important biblical texts for insight into the person of the Holy Spirit caused me to look at the Spirit in fresh ways, yet this masterful study also bolstered my confidence in the historic Christian consensus. *Who Is the Holy Spirit?* is ideal for scholars, students, and church leaders alike. I highly recommend it."

—*Matt Pinson, president, Welch College*

"Who is the Holy Spirit? brings a biblically-rich look at the third person of the Trinity in a way that is accessible to the lay person or the pastor. I am thankful for Dr. Yarnell's scholarship, but also for his passion for the life and work of the Holy Spirit."

—*Ed Stetzer, dean of the School of Mission, Ministry and Leadership, Billy Graham Chair of Church, Mission and Evangelism, executive director, Billy Graham Center, Wheaton College*

"As an evangelical, I am grateful for the increased interest in the person of the Holy Spirit. As a Baptist, I am even more appreciative that one of our leading theologians now adds his voice to teach the church about Him. In this latest volume of the Hobbs College Library, Malcolm Yarnell provides a theological account of the person of the Holy Spirit through the interpretation of six biblical passages. Yarnell's calling as pastor-theologian shines through as he seeks throughout the volume not only to teach the reader about the Spirit but also to encourage the reader to trust, engage, and even worship the Holy Spirit. This work will equip pastors well as they build up God's church."

—*Keith Whitfield, vice president for academic administration, dean of graduate studies, associate professor of theology, Southeastern Baptist Theological Seminary*

Commendations for Hobbs College Library

"This series honors a wonderful servant of Christ with a stellar lineup of contributors. What a gift to the body of Christ! My hope and prayer is that it will be widely read and used for the glory of God and the good of his Church."

—Daniel L. Akin, president, Southeastern Baptist Theological Seminary

"This series is a must have, go-to resource for everyone who is serious about Bible study, teaching, and preaching. The authors are committed to the authority of the Bible and the vitality of the local church. I am excited about the kingdom impact of this much needed resource."

—Hance Dilbeck, executive director, Baptist General Convention of Oklahoma

"I am very excited about the dynamic leadership of Dr. Heath Thomas and his vision of the Hobbs College Library at Oklahoma Baptist University that he is developing. Through his work as Dean of the Hobbs College of Theology, this 21-volume set of books will ascend the theological understanding of laypeople, church leaders, pastors, and bi-vocational pastors. Therefore, I want to encourage you to participate in this vision that will equip your church to make a greater difference for Jesus Christ in your community and around the world."

—Ronnie Floyd, senior pastor, Cross Church, Northwest AR, and president, the
  Southern Baptist Convention Executive Committee

"This series offers an outstanding opportunity for leaders of all kind to strengthen their knowledge of God, his word, and the manner in which we should engage the culture around us. Do not miss this opportunity to grow as a disciple of Jesus and as a leader of his church."

—Micah Fries, senior pastor, Brainerd Baptist Church, Chattanooga, TN

"The Hobbs College Library is a perfect way to help people who want to grow in the basics of their faith. Whether you are a layperson or longtime pastor, this tool will help give you the theological base needed for ministry today. I highly recommend this tremendous resource to anyone wanting to deepen their understanding of Scripture."

—Jack Graham, pastor, Prestonwood Baptist Church, North TX, and former
  president, the Southern Baptist Convention

"The best resources are those that develop the church theologically while instructing her practically in the work of the Great Commission. Dr. Thomas has assembled an impressive host of contributors for a new set of resources that will equip leaders at all levels who want to leave a lasting impact for the gospel. Dr. Hobbs exemplified the pastor-leader-theologian, and it's inspiring to see a series put out in his name that so aptly embodies his ministry and calling."

—J.D. Greear, pastor, The Summit Church, Raleigh-Durham, NC, and president, the
  Southern Baptist Convention

WHO IS THE
HOLY SPIRIT?

WHO IS THE HOLY SPIRIT?

*Biblical Insights into
His Divine Person*

MALCOLM B. YARNELL III

HEATH A. THOMAS, *Editor*

OBU

ACADEMIC
NASHVILLE, TENNESSEE

Dedicated to

one who knows and loves God the Holy Spirit,

Karen Annette Searcy Yarnell

Contents

Contents

About the Library

T he Hobbs College Library equips Christians with tools for growing in the faith and for effective ministry. The library trains its readers in three major areas: Bible, theology, and ministry. The series originates from the Herschel H. Hobbs College of Theology and Ministry at Oklahoma Baptist University, where biblical, orthodox, and practical education lies at its core. Training the next generation was important for the great Baptist statesman Dr. Herschel H. Hobbs, and the Hobbs College that bears his name fosters that same vision.

The Hobbs College Library: Biblical. Orthodox. Practical.

Preface

Q uestions, questions, questions. Perhaps the best way to preface this book is by answering the questions posed about it by colleagues, family, and friends.

First, there have been questions about the subject matter. "What is your book about?" my youngest daughter asked me.

I told her the title is *Who Is the Holy Spirit?*

"Why did you choose that subject?"

"Well," I said, "most things written about the Holy Spirit for a good while now have focused on what the Holy Spirit does rather than who he is."

She immediately responded, "Sometimes it is difficult to speak about 'origin.' It is easier to talk about what somebody does than what somebody is. But what somebody does tells you about who they are."

My wife and I stared at each other in wonder at this little girl's ability to think so deeply. But Elizabeth was not finished.

"It is like trying to define 'energy,'" she went on. "We know what energy can cause, but we have a more difficult time saying what energy is. So, we look at what energy is doing; then we try to say from that what energy is. But we don't really know what energy is." I am still amazed at how my daughter expressed so simply a solution to the complex problem of the relationship between the economic and the ontological.[1] She likewise proposed analogy as the solution to the problem of language about God.[2] Finally, she illustrated the correlation between unseen power and the Spirit. And she just turned twelve!

That little episode indicates that our young people are thinking deep thoughts. And we who are their elders must help them see how Scripture has the answers to the greatest problems in human life. This book attempts to help you see who the Holy Spirit is through sacred Scripture's description of him. It may be classified as an exercise in "biblical theology," or more appropriately, as "theological interpretation," although its subject is limited and its audience is more popular. Therefore, we refer to it as an exercise in garnering biblical insights into the identity of the third person of the Trinity.

As an exercise in theological interpretation, this book employs a form of argument that could be described as "from a biblical conviction according to a text-driven method for an ultimate goal": The "conviction" is that Scripture is the perfect source for understanding ultimate reality, in this case for perceiving the identity of the Holy Spirit. The "method" is to allow the canonical text, assisted by historic orthodox exegesis, to drive the theology that will help preachers and teachers explain to their students and congregations the meaning of the reality of the Holy Spirit. The "goal" is to encourage the true worship of God by his redeemed human creatures in Christ through the guidance of the Holy Spirit.

---

[1] On the problem of the "economic Trinity," which considers the works of the Trinity, in relationship to the "ontological Trinity" or "eternal Trinity," which deals with the being and persons of God, see my *God the Trinity: Biblical Portraits* (Nashville: B&H Academic, 2016).

[2] On the problem of theological language, see my essay "Systematic Theology," in *Theology, Church, and Ministry: A Handbook of Theological Education*, ed. David S. Dockery (Nashville: B&H Academic, 2017), 257–80.

A second major question has been, "Why did you choose to write this book now?" My reasoning has to do with a measurable lacuna, or absence, in the existing literature. During and after the Reformation, teaching about the Holy Spirit among orthodox Protestants was primarily concerned with the human person's justification. After the eighteenth-century evangelical revivals, the attention shifted, this time toward the doctrine of sanctification. Yet later, after the rise of Pentecostalism in the early twentieth century, most Western Christian traditions paid significant attention to the work of the Spirit in its more spectacular manifestations, including the practices of speaking in tongues, healing, and prophecy.

If the Reformers and their evangelical heirs focused on the internal work of the Spirit in salvation and sanctification, modern Pentecostals and their charismatic heirs focused on external signs and wonders. Alas, in the midst of these widespread renewals of pneumatologic thought and practice, little attention has been paid to identifying the *person* of the Holy Spirit. This is a deeply problematic oversight, because *who the Holy Spirit is*, as my daughter intuited, determines *what the Holy Spirit does*. This book seeks to rectify a widespread knowledge gap by answering the question, Who is the Holy Spirit?

A third question has been, "For whom are you writing this book?" It has been a great joy to create this manuscript at the invitation of Dr. Heath Thomas, dean of the Herschel H. Hobbs College of Theology and Ministry at Oklahoma Baptist University. In one of his many helpful lay commentaries on the Bible, Hobbs wrote, "The study of this gospel will prove to be a rich and rewarding experience."[3] I can still remember as if it were yesterday when that great

---

[3] Herschel H. Hobbs, *The Gospel of John: A Study Guide* (Grand Rapids: Zondervan, 1965), 7.

expositor granted me the "rich and rewarding experience" of hearing him preach the gospel. Hobbs delivered a sermon that brought three men to faith that evening—an elderly man; a young, rebellious man; and a boy. At the very same time, that venerable pastor engaged this young theologian's inquisitive mind.

Hobbs's awe-inspiring ability to hold every listener's attention came from his continual effort to exposit Scripture, coupled with a genuine pastoral care for every human being.[4] Hobbs understood the human condition as well as the divine emolument. He could speak to large and diverse audiences with illustrative words and cognitive concepts that both evangelized the nonbeliever and instructed the believer. My ministry has been shaped by that experience at Hobbs's feet, for I determined also to feed the mature while helping the immature come to faith. Hobbs was a widely respected Baptist pastor-theologian deemed at the time, and rightly so, to be without peer. I hope the now-departed Oklahoma Baptist pastor would have approved of the effort by an academic pastor-theologian in this book to speak about the person of the Holy Spirit in a simultaneously true and compelling way for a diverse and needy audience.

Keywords: Holy Spirit; God; person

Malcolm B. Yarnell III
Markum Ranch Estates, Texas

---

[4] Concerning Hobbs as a pastor-theologian, see James Leo Garrett Jr., "Herschel Harold Hobbs: Pastoral and Denominational Expositor-Theologian," *Southwestern Journal of Theology* 54 no. 2 (Spring 2012): 132–40.

Introduction

O ur purpose herein is to answer the question, Who is the Holy
Spirit? In the midst of discovering an answer to that query,
we shall consider six grand vistas of the biblical revelation. The
first three presentations of the Spirit's identity derive from the Old
Testament. The way Israel perceived the Spirit lays the necessary
foundation upon which the church must construct any proper
doctrine of the Holy Spirit. However, a truly Christian doctrine of
the Spirit must also reflect the reality of the progression between the
covenants. There is a profound difference between how the divine
Spirit related to ancient Israel and how he relates to the church of
Jesus Christ. The key to understanding that difference rests in the
crucible of the exalted person and the saving work of Jesus Christ.
He is the only person who baptizes with the Spirit. Therefore, after
considering how the Spirit was known to Moses, Samuel, and David,
we must turn to the revelation of the Spirit granted to Matthew, John,
and Paul. If the Lord, who is the Spirit, so wills, a careful study of
the teachings of these great prophets and apostles, whom the Holy
Spirit inspired in speech and text, should allow us to perceive the
same Spirit, who is God.

Before we address the biblical identity of the Holy Spirit, I must
first make a couple of admissions. First and foremost, I presume that
the Word of God provides us with trustworthy information regarding

who God is, who Jesus is, and who the Holy Spirit is. I hope, in a forthcoming book, to address the doctrines of God and of God's revelation with more depth than this book allows (and have elsewhere already addressed these doctrines, in summary fashion). Until that time, we will here assume that Scripture in its original autographs is without error and that the texts the church now possesses are infallibly able to convey God's will for human conduct and his way for our salvation. God's Word is perfect and sufficient, living and active, and instructive and applicable. This means the Bible, as a diverse yet united canon inspired by the Holy Spirit, will remain our primary interactive text throughout this book.

Second, I admittedly write from within a certain tradition. However, denominational commitment does not mean one should needlessly restrict one's ideas only to the teachers in one's own tradition. The larger witness of Israel and of the church, both in Scripture and in the interpretation of Scripture through the ages, must be taken into account. If we do not listen to the voices of the saints who have come before us or who speak elsewhere among the churches today, our doctrine of the Holy Spirit will be unduly impoverished. In his famous Corinthian correspondence, Paul twice emphasized a universal Christian truth: As an individual Christian, he said, "I also have the Holy Spirit" (1 Cor 7:40). As a church teacher, he said, "We have the same Spirit of faith" (2 Cor 4:13). Paul thereby taught that the Holy Spirit does not belong exclusively to any one teacher or to any one church. Rather, the same Spirit of God permeates and rules all of his churches.

Though I typically write in an academic style, my purpose here requires a slightly different manner of speaking. My goal is to speak plainly yet instructively to the average Christian preacher or teacher about the Spirit of God. Those interested in a higher academic study, who wish to penetrate into the dogma of the Holy Spirit with more technical accuracy, are encouraged to consult my long essay on the person and work of the Spirit in Daniel Akin's *A Theology for the Church*.[1] In this work, although I will not say everything possible about the Spirit, I will say much that is important. Instead, I hope to help clarify for the preacher in the pulpit, the teacher behind the podium, and ultimately, the average Christian in the pew, who the Holy Spirit is. That is, I wish to leave a good impression of the Spirit's person and character from the biblical text. This goal requires not a universal systematic account but a more popular interpretative account.

Finally, the ultimate purpose for this study about the Holy Spirit is not to satisfy curiosity, but to encourage worship. Yes, I hope that while reading this book, you will intellectually know more than you knew before about who the Holy Spirit is. However, even as you build a better base of biblical knowledge, I hope you will be compelled by the same Spirit to devote yourself to God more than you did previously. My prayer is that every person who reads this book will be prompted to thank God for the gift of his Spirit even as they worship God in Christ. Moreover, I hope that by discovering how divine and how personal the Holy Spirit really is, you will be compelled not only to worship God *in* the Spirit, but to worship God *as* the Spirit. My oldest daughter, Kathryn, who is fourteen, recently asked me, "So, Dad, do we worship the Spirit? Or, do we worship through the Spirit?" My answer was, "Both." Her heartwarming and enthusiastic response was one of joyous discovery. May yours be likewise.

---

[1] Malcolm B. Yarnell III, "The Person and Work of the Holy Spirit," in *A Theology for the Church*, ed. Daniel L. Akin, rev. ed. (Nashville: B&H Academic, 2014), 483–540.

CHAPTER 1

Where Do We Begin?
Insights from Genesis 1

D on't you think a good place to begin most any story is at the
beginning? If so, then the beginning of Scripture is the best
place to begin answering the question, Who is the Holy Spirit? A
Latin loanword from the Greek, *Genesis* means "beginnings." The
first book of the Bible was apparently named Genesis because it
concerns the source or origin both of the universe and of Israel. And
at the beginning of the biblical book of Genesis, we find the first
occurrences of two extremely important theological words, *God*
(Heb. *Elohim*) and *Spirit* (Heb. *Ruah*). The word for God appears
in the first verse and the word for Spirit appears in the second verse.

Beginning our discussion of the identity of the Holy Spirit at
the beginning of Scripture is a decision easily made. But following
through with a widely accepted interpretation immediately entan-
gles us in a history of vigorous debate about the meaning of *Ruah* in
Gen 1:2. Both Jewish and Christian interpreters have divided over
exactly how to interpret this important foundational text. When a
significant passage like this generates great debate, we must ultimately fall back on the hermeneutical axiom that Scripture remains
the best interpreter of Scripture. Another way to state this is that the
clearer texts within Scripture, especially when written by the same
human author or in the same genre, shed light on the texts that are

less clear to our eyes. As we interpret Genesis 1, then, we shall— we must—consult other biblical passages. In doing so, this text will teach us much about the Holy Spirit: specifically, that

- the Spirit is mysterious,
- the Spirit is the Mover, and
- the Spirit is mighty.

The Spirit Is Mysterious

The context for the first appearance of the *Ruah Elohim,* "Spirit of God," must be taken into consideration. Several words are used to describe the setting in which the Spirit first appears. Genesis 1:1 states, "In the beginning God created the heavens and the earth." Verse 2 continues, "Now the earth was formless and empty, darkness covered the surface of the watery depths." The words translated as "formless" and "empty" and "darkness" all convey the same idea, that created things were lacking. There was nothing, because there was no form and no content and no light. The Hebrew *tohu* may be translated as "formless" or "desert" or even "chaos." The Hebrew *bohu* may be translated as "void" or "wasteland." And the Hebrew *khoshek* may be translated as "darkness" or "night." These words are not intended to indicate precision regarding present states of existence. Instead, they reinforce one another to indicate that there was no existence of anything whatsoever, except for that which preexisted creation, namely, at this point in the text, God and his *Ruah.*

The indefinite nature of creation at this seminal moment compels us to consider that God and his *Ruah* should not be defined by things that exist. This is because, besides God, nothing else as yet existed! There is nothing to which we can compare God because there was nothing else in existence before God and His Spirit and

His Word created it. *Tohu* and *khoshek* also appear in Isa 45:18–19, where God's creative activity is likewise expressed as the opposite of emptiness and darkness. God formed and made the earth precisely so it would "not . . . be a wasteland." Nor was the earth intended to be "a land of darkness." Deuteronomy 32:10 strikes a similar theme in its discussion of God's intention for his people. God took Israel out of the wasteland to himself. So, if there was nothing in the beginning, then when God created, he created *that which is* out of *that which was not*. This reminds us of the classical Christian doctrine that God created everything *ex nihilo*, "out of nothing" (cf. Rom 4:17).

So, what, if anything, can Gen 1:2 tell us positively about the *Ruah* of God? Well, definitively, it tells us nothing positive except that he simply is when nothing else is. There was no way to explain God and his Spirit with reference to something else, when as yet there existed nothing else.[1] There was no analogy of God or of his Spirit available yet in existence. The analogy will come later in Genesis 1, with the creation of the ones made in the image of God. Moreover, this is not the only mystery that this verse provides us about *Ruah Elohim*, "the Spirit of God."

A second mystery about the *Ruah* in Gen 1:2 relates to the proper interpretation of the word *ruah* itself. Technically, *ruah* may be interpreted in either a natural sense or supernatural sense. It could thus mean anything from "wind" to "breath" to "spirit." In addition, the second word, *Elohim*, has been translated here not only as "God," but also as "mighty." Thus, commentators have offered translations everywhere from the theologically assertive "Spirit of God" to the theologically vague "wind from God" to the theologically vacuous

---

[1] For New Testament passages that undergird the orthodox creedal doctrine that God created the world *ex nihilo*, "out of nothing," see Romans 4:11 and Hebrews 11:3.

"mighty wind." The most descriptive translations from a theological perspective are either "Spirit of God," which emphasizes the being of God, or "breath of God," which emphasizes the activity of God. Help in interpreting this text again will come from how the term might be best interpreted in the context of the biblical canon, especially within the book of Genesis itself.

In Gen 2:7, *nephesh*, "being," and *neshamah*, "breath," two terms closely related to *ruah*, since *ruah* also may indicate being and breath, are used to indicate the direct activity of God in bringing about human life. God breathed life itself into the human body such that man became a living being. Being so close to Gen 2:7, and ensconced between the obviously divine meanings of *Elohim* in Gen 1:1 and 1:3, Gen 1:2 is doubtless not to be taken as a weak attributive adjective derived from God's sovereignty, "mighty," but as a strongly substantive noun, "God." Excluding "mighty wind" as an unfit translation for the context leaves us with the two major options for translating *Ruah Elohim*: either one of the more personal meanings, "Spirit of God" or "breath of God," or the less personal meaning of "wind from God." But which of the two remaining primary possibilities is best?

In Gen 6:3, *Ruah* also appears with God as the One in possession of *Ruah*. Reflecting back on his breathing the gift of life in Gen 2:7 and his warning to humanity in Gen 2:17 that he would bring death for disobedience, God then decided to remove his gift of life from humanity in Gen 6:3: "And the LORD said, 'My Spirit will not remain with mankind forever, because they are corrupt.'" The noun *ruah* here, as in many other places, could be translated with a personalized "breath" as well as "spirit." In Gen 6:3, *ruah* also has a suffix for the personal singular possessive, meaning "my," attached to it. So, *ruah* in this case is directly identified by God as belonging to himself—"my Spirit" or "my breath." With such a strong form

8

of self-identification between God and his *Ruah* in Gen 6:3, it becomes very likely that *Ruah* in Gen 1:2 should also be taken in one of the personal senses—"Spirit of God" or "breath of God." While the weaker translations are technically possible, the canonical context, especially in the early chapters of Genesis, points to a personal identification between God and his Spirit. The best translation of *Ruah Elohim* in Gen 1:2, especially if we take it as a reference substantively to his person rather than less substantively, though still personally, to his activity, therefore, remains "Spirit of God."

On the one hand, the Spirit remains mysterious from the perspective of positive definition in Gen 1:2, due to the lack of a positive analogy from creation, at least at the time to which Gen 1:2 refers. On the other hand, the mystery of the Spirit does not extend to the divine identity of the Spirit. The *Ruah Elohim* of Gen 1:2 is definitely the Spirit who is in some significant way closely identified with God himself. He is substantively and personally the Spirit *of God*. He is not a mere metaphor for a created activity or, even worse, for a created identity.

The Spirit Is the Mover

In a most interesting choice of terms, Moses described the Holy Spirit as "hovering over the surface of the waters" (Gen 1:2). The connotations that arise from the use of the Hebrew participle *marahepet* (derived from the verb *rahap*), will have a long-term impact on the way the Holy Spirit is described in the rest of Scripture. But the verb and its derivatives are only used three times in the Old Testament. Deuteronomy 32:11 uses a similar verbal form as that in Gen 1:2 (the Piel stem). In a different verbal form (the Qal stem), Jer 23:9 describes the true prophet's bones as "trembl[ing]" at the preaching of the false prophets.

The song of Moses in Deut 32 says that the Lord "watches over his nest like an eagle and hovers [*rahep*] over his young" (v. 11). In Ugaritic, a Semitic language that is very similar to ancient Hebrew, the verb *rahap* is always used to describe the activity of an eagle or eagles in "soaring" or "hovering." The parallel verb of *'ur* in Deut 32:11, also used of an eagle, indicates that the Lord glided above his people in the wilderness to guide them and protect them. Due to these biblical and linguistic associations, ancient Jewish commentators correlated the Spirit with the *shekinah* glory of God, which was evident in "the pillar of cloud by day and the pillar of fire by night" and moved over God's people in their wilderness journeys (Exod 13:21–22; 14:19–20). According to the rabbis, the *shekinah* glory of God was also seen in the temple during the reign of Solomon (2 Chr 7:1–3).

For these reasons, we may associate the activity of the Spirit in Gen 1:2 with the nurturing activity of God in Deut 32 and Exodus 13–14. According to Gen 1:2, at the cusp of creation, the Spirit of God hovered over the surface of the waters for the purpose of guiding his creation and protecting it. The Spirit acts in this way to move creation to become that which God wants it to become. This description carries not only a sense of guidance over a process and protection of a formation, but also a sense of transcendence and immanence at the same time. The Spirit of God is sovereign over all creatures and the progress of creatures in time, and yet he is intimately involved with his creatures and their progress.

While the Spirit stood above creation as Creator, he was directly involved with creation as providential Guide. In a colloquial way, we might say that the Holy Spirit is the "Mover and Shaker" who directed creation into existence, guiding it and protecting it as it grew, hovering above its progress as an adult eagle would hover over its young. (Similarly, one may perceive the Word's coordinate instrumentality in bringing creation into existence through a canonical comparison of Gen 1:3 with John 1:3, Col 1:16, and Heb 1:2.) The Holy Spirit moves like a bird of prey, powerful in his dominating presence in the skies. And like a bird of preparation, he protects and provides for his young progeny as they mature. The appearance of the Holy Spirit in the form of a "dove" will occur later, but the association of the Spirit with these majestic birdlike qualities arises at the beginning of Scripture.

The Spirit Is Mighty

The unwary reader may presume that the Spirit is somehow weak or insubstantial due to his metaphorical association with a bird. This could not be further from the truth. The Spirit of God is mighty like God, because He is identified with God. Both the Old Testament and the New Testament teach that the Spirit of God has the power of God. This can be seen in the Spirit's roles in the major activities of God, such as the three divine activities of the creation of life, of providence over the progress of life, and of the creation of new life.

First, Scripture is clear, from Genesis 1 forward, that the Spirit of God is active in the creation of life. The Spirit carefully stands over that which is not yet, bringing creation into being (Gen 1:2) due to the will of God (v. 1) that was spoken by God (v. 3). According to the psalmist, both the Word of God and the Spirit of God were necessary for the creation of the universe: "The heavens were made by the word of the LORD, and all the stars, by the breath [*Ruah*, Spirit] of his mouth" (Ps 33:6). Again, referring to the creatures on the earth, the psalmist wrote, "When you send your breath [*Ruah*, Spirit], they are created, and you renew the surface of the ground" (Ps 104:30). In particular, the breath of the human being is entirely dependent upon the creating and sustaining breath of God himself.

When God's Spirit moves mightily in personal creation, life comes to humanity (Gen 2:7; Job 33:4). As long as God's Spirit sustains his or her breath, life remains in the human being (Gen 6:3; Job 27:3). But when God's Spirit withdraws himself, human life ceases (Job 34:14–15; Ps 104:29).

Second, the Spirit of God is active in governing the progress of human life throughout history. The Spirit is sovereign in his movement within the human life. He cannot be controlled by the human being, but, like the natural wind, the Spirit "blows where [he] pleases" (John 3:8). The Spirit is obliquely referred to as the "finger of God" (Exod 8:19; 31:18; Luke 11:30), indicating personal might, and has power to change the spiritual tenor of the human being (Matt 12:28, 31; Luke 11:13). The Holy Spirit also sovereignly decides exactly how he will manifest himself in the dispersal of spiritual gifts within the church (1 Cor 12:11). For the good of the world, the Spirit restrains evil within the human community so that its destructive power may not yet be fully realized (2 Thess 2:6–7). We may thus argue, through such texts in the biblical canon, that God works everywhere in the history of humanity through his Spirit.

Third, the Spirit of God is active in the creation of new life. Due to the fall of humanity, a fall in which all of us participated through Adam, we brought upon ourselves the sentence of death. Death is the judgment of God upon humanity for our sins. However, God also loves us and wants to show us mercy. God, therefore, out of love, sent his Son to become a human being, Jesus Christ, in order to live the perfect life and to die a substitutionary death on the cross. He arose from the dead, making the way for us, through faith in him, into eternal life. However, we cannot receive the renewing or regenerating work of God in our lives apart from the Holy Spirit. The regenerative work of the Spirit was prophesied in Ezekiel's vision of the valley of dry bones. That prophecy concludes, "I will put my

Spirit in you, and you will live" (Ezek 37:14). Later, Jesus explained that the new birth cannot happen apart from the work of the Holy Spirit (John 3:5–8).

From these biblical texts, among many others, we can see that the Holy Spirit is mighty with regard to life. He creates life. He guides life. He re-creates life. He created life out of nothing. He sustains life and guides it according to God's purposes. He regenerates the fallen human being through the gifts of faith and repentance, which the human being must receive from God in order to be saved. The Nicene Creed, revised at the Council of Constantinople in 381, echoes the teaching of Jesus. In John 6:63, Jesus said that "the Spirit is the one who gives life." The Nicene Creed, therefore, confesses on behalf of all orthodox Christians that the Holy Spirit is the "Life-giver."[2] The Holy Spirit is mighty to give life in the first place, to sustain human life in history, and to give new life to sinners who believe in Jesus.

Summary

From Gen 1:2 we learned that the Spirit is mysterious in his exact identity, but God has revealed enough to let us know that the Spirit is "of God." We also learned from this foundational text that the Spirit moves in creation and in providence. Finally, we learned that the Spirit is mighty in his power—He is sovereign over creation, over the progress of human lives, and over the merciful gift of renewed life. A partial answer to the larger question, Who is the Holy Spirit? is, therefore, that he is mysterious, that he moves, and that he is mighty.

---

[2] See the new translation of the Nicene Creed in Malcolm B. Yarnell III, *God the Trinity: Biblical Portraits* (Nashville: B&H Academic, 2016), 241.

But can we say more regarding the relationship of the Holy Spirit to God? Theologian Colin Gunton concluded from a strict reading of Gen 1:2 that, "while we cannot say categorically that this refers to the Spirit we know as the Holy Spirit, we should not be afraid to understand it trinitarianly in the light of later thought. This is justifiable particularly in view of the fact that other Old Testament uses of the same expression clearly refer to the Spirit."[3] Gunton is correct to be circumspect in his reading of Gen 1:2, but he also properly perceives a trinitarian meaning in light of the canon as a whole. We have discussed some of those other uses of *Ruah*, but now we turn to a very enlightening historical text that tells us a great deal more about the identity of the Spirit of God.

---

[3] Colin E. Gunton, *The Triune Creator: A Historical and Systematic Study*, Edinburgh Studies in Constructive Theology (Edinburgh: Edinburgh University Press, 1998), 17.

CHAPTER 2

Is the Spirit Also the Sovereign Lord God? Insights from 1 Samuel 10–19

A s the Old Testament progresses, it tells us ever more about God himself, as well as about angels, humanity, and other creatures. The Old Testament also describes the relationships that various individuals—divine, angelic, and human—have with one another. One of the most important questions before us now, especially after seeing his prominence in Genesis 1, concerns the relationship of the Spirit to the Lord God. In particular, we must address whether the Old Testament, like the New Testament, teaches that the Spirit is also the sovereign Lord God together with the Father and the Son.

Genesis 1:2 alludes to the deity and the personhood of the Holy Spirit in the way that the text correlates the Spirit to *Elohim*. Later, the allusions become more explicit. However, these truths must still be perceived by the human being. While human perception of deep theological truth through revelation is the result of a divine gift, there is also substantial literary evidence on behalf of mere logic affirming the deity and the personhood of the Holy Spirit in the Old Testament. Indeed, in the inspired historical book that we now call 1 Samuel, the Holy Spirit is identified as the Lord God himself.

But this identification often occurs obliquely and so subtly that the unwary may never see it.

A cursory summary of 1 Samuel will be helpful as we begin.[1] The early chapters are devoted to the birth and anointing of the last great judge, Samuel, who was also a prophet and a priest. Chapters 8–15 recount the development of kingship and the history of the reign of Saul, the first king of Israel. Saul's story is enlightening for a doctrine of the Holy Spirit because of how the Spirit worked in his life. Chapters 16–19 shift from being primarily concerned about Saul to narrating how David was chosen by God. The transition in kingship depends upon a shift in the activity of the Spirit. Finally, chapters 20–31 disclose how David ultimately came to replace Saul. From the perspective of the doctrine of the Spirit, the narratives of chapters 10, 11, 16, 18, and 19 are particularly instructive. The Spirit of God in 1 Samuel involves himself intimately in the lives of Israel's leaders, empowering them for service, working within their hearts, and sovereignly guiding their path.

Soon after God's people entered the promised land, there was a time when Israel was not ruled by a unitary mediator. Before this period, Moses and Joshua were the singularly prominent leaders, as were the Israelite kings after this period. During the intervening period between the singular leaders, the Israelite tribes were ruled more immediately by God. When he deemed it necessary, God spontaneously raised up various "judges" to assist his people. In times of danger and distress, he gave these judges power to deliver Israel from foreign oppression. For instance, the Spirit of the Lord came directly upon judges such as Othniel, Gideon, and Jephthah to empower them for victory over Israel's opponents, thus ensuring

---

[1] For further theological insights from the books of Samuel, please consider Heath Thomas and J. D. Greear, *Exalting Jesus in 1 & 2 Samuel*, Christ-Centered Exposition Commentary (Nashville: Holman Reference, 2016).

peace for a time (Judg 3:10–11; 6:34; 8:28; 11:29). These judges understood that the Lord, rather than a human king, actually ruled the nation (8:22–23). Unfortunately, in spite of the presence of the Spirit working through them, the judges were not immune from displaying personal failure even in the midst of public triumph (8:24–27; 11:29–31).

The most spectacular personality among Israel's judges was Samson. It is remarkable that the Spirit of God would rush repeatedly upon Samuel in power, typically before a mighty act of rescue (14:6, 19; 15:14). So, the Spirit of God gave the judges power to perform their important, if temporary and noninheritable, office of leadership.[2] With the rise of the kings, some aspects of leadership changed. Unlike the judges in prior centuries, the kings were considered permanent, and their children might inherit their office.

The Spirit empowered both the judges and the kings to fulfill their offices, but the office of judge and the office of king differed significantly. Most importantly, on the one hand, the judges were earlier authorized to lead temporarily through charismatic identification. That is, the Spirit graciously empowered them to deliver God's people from tribulation, and the people immediately recognized the direct divine gifting through the judges' powerful actions. Such dramatic influence did not, however, translate into the building of a personal dynasty. On the other hand, the kings and their descendants might continue to rule for a time even when they were personally in rebellion against the Spirit. The relationship between the Spirit and the kings was, as a result, more complex and, therefore, more enlightening.

---

[2] The Spirit did not necessarily come upon a judge due to his holiness or worthiness, but by sheer grace.

In the following review of the 1 Samuel narrative, which focuses on the development of Israelite kingship, we shall see that

- the Spirit is God,
- the Spirit is sovereign, and
- the Spirit is the Lord.

The Spirit Is God

So, why did the monarchical form of rule develop? The people of Israel had noticed how their surrounding enemies functioned with kings and were often successful. In a pragmatic, worldly mode of thinking, they presumed the establishment of a monarchy would also grant them better rule and military victory (1 Sam 8:5). And because the people were depending on human means rather than on divine guidance, the Lord informed Samuel, "They have not rejected you; they have rejected me as their king" (8:7). Nevertheless, in spite of their rejection of God's direct rule, the Lord showed them mercy and decided to bless their requested form of governance. But Samuel warned them there would be difficulties with the new system (8:11–18).

Afterwards, the three anointed offices in ancient Israel became that of king, priest, and prophet, later known as the *triplex munus*, or threefold office.[3] Samuel, the last of the judges, was both a leading

---

[3] The tripartite scheme of prophet, priest, and king was perhaps first noticed among Christians by Eusebius of Caesarea (*Ecclesiastical History*, 1.3.8). Following the ruminations of John Calvin (*Institutes of the Christian Religion*, 2.15) and other Reformers, the concept became a theological axiom. Christ Jesus was seen as the inheritor of all three of the major Israelite offices, otherwise known as *triplex munus Christi*, "the threefold office of Christ." Due to the widespread usage of this threefold paradigm in contemporary literature, the office of judge is not ascribed to Christ as prominently as it probably should be.

priest and one of the great prophets in the land. The first king whom God chose for Israel through Samuel was Saul, the son of Kish, of the small tribe of Benjamin. As will become evident, the priestly and prophetic offices, herein held by Samuel, were intended to coexist and function alongside the kingly office of Saul. While it seems providentially designed to serve as a means for restraining monarchical corruption and abuse, this system of distinct offices was almost immediately subverted by the first occupant of the royal throne. The prophetic office might be shared by kings and priests, but the priestly and royal offices were typically intended to remain separate in ancient Israel.[4]

The Lord chose to prepare the king for his office of kingship inwardly through the empowering work of his Spirit, evidenced through anointing. Samuel's act of pouring oil, or anointing, was the Lord's formal and visible declaration that Saul would be king over Israel (1 Sam 10:1). The Hebrew word for "anoint," *mashah*, popularly transliterated as "Messiah," was later translated into the Greek New Testament as *Christos*, "Christ." The outward action of pouring oil, or anointing, was paralleled by the movement of the Spirit of God. The ceremonial form for anointing paradigmatically included the outward anointing, a description of the Spirit's working in the king's life, and a call to obey the Lord in his actions. The call to obedience given to Saul included a reminder that it was necessary for Saul to "wait" on the priest, Samuel, before offering a sacrifice (10:1, 6–8).

It is with the Spirit's working upon the king that we are primarily concerned. The text itself reads, "The Spirit of the LORD will come powerfully on you, you will prophesy with them [the

---

[4] Perhaps with Christological foresight, David sometimes violated the distinction, as when he ate the showbread.

prophets], and you will be transformed" (10:6). Samuel's promise of the Spirit's work included four components in verses 6–8: the coming of the Spirit, the report of revelation, the recipient's internal transformation, and the presence of the Spirit. The first three of these four components were explicitly fulfilled in the life of Saul, thereby verifying that the Lord had chosen Saul to lead the people as king. The fourth component is described a few verses later. It introduces a theme that will build in importance throughout 1 Samuel and the rest of Scripture.

The first component happened according to Samuel's promise, "the Spirit of the LORD will come powerfully upon you." The Hebrew verb *tsalah*, "to prosper" or "to come upon," indicates either a powerful rushing upon a person or thing or the giving of success to a person. The Spirit of God is said to have rushed powerfully upon the judge Samson (noted earlier); upon the first king, Saul (1 Sam 10:10; 11:6); and upon the second king, David (16:13). The same verb was similarly used by the prophet Amos to describe the coming of "the LORD" in power upon human beings (Amos 5:6).[5] Therefore, when *tsalah* is used to describe the coming of the Spirit of God upon the king, it indicates that God's sovereign power moves through the office of the king.

The second component of Samuel's promise regarding the Spirit in the life of the new king was that Saul would "prophesy with" other prophets. And when Saul first encountered a group of prophets after Samuel's promise, "the Spirit of God came powerfully on him, and he prophesied along with them" (1 Sam 10:10). The outward change in Saul's behavior was a shock for those who knew the previously retiring young man. They coined a phrase that

---

[5] *Tsalah* is used a little later in 1 Samuel of the movement of an evil spirit upon Saul (1 Sam 18:10).

was widely repeated, "Is Saul also among the prophets?" (10:12). In spite of scholarly assumptions to the contrary, there is no indication in this text that Saul's experience was an ecstatic trance. It simply says Saul "prophesied." He spoke the word of the Lord as part of a group. He was not even the leader of the prophets, but only "among" them. We are not told what he spoke as part of this ensemble; only that he spoke among them. The Spirit led the first king of Israel to proclaim the word of God as well as lead the people of God. Among God's people, prophetic proclamation and royal leadership remained corollaries.

The third component of Samuel's description of how the Spirit would work in Saul's anointing to the office of king was the promise that he would "be transformed" (10:6). The sentence, more fully, says that Saul would be changed to *'ish 'aher*, "another person." Some clarifications are required. First, the Spirit's transformation of Saul does not mean the man would lose control of himself. Instead, he would be "equipped with power to play a new role."[6] Second, from a New Testament perspective, we might presume that the transforming work of the Spirit in a person's life necessarily entails personal salvation. However, there is no indication that Saul was saved here. Rather, the Spirit of God came upon Saul to prepare him to function as a king. To read anything more than that into the text is to go beyond what the Old Testament actually says.

In what way was Saul inwardly transformed by the Spirit? If the alteration of Saul did not necessarily entail his being "born again" (as in John 3), then how was Saul's character changed? First Samuel 11 provides us a clue as to what Samuel's promise regarding Saul's internal change meant. Where this retiring giant had once hidden in

---

[6] David Toshio Tsumura, *The First Book of Samuel*, New International Commentary on the Old Testament (Grand Rapids: Eerdmans, 2007), 288.

the baggage rather than face the people (10:21–22), Saul was later compelled to take very bold and very public action. For example, soon after hearing of the threat to the inhabitants of Jabesh-Gilead, "the Spirit of God suddenly came powerfully on him, and his anger burned furiously" (11:6). Compelled internally, Saul cut up oxen and sent the pieces throughout Israel, threatening retaliation if the rest of the tribes did not come to the aid of Jabesh-Gilead. Saul's heart of timid trepidation was changed to one of decisive resolve. "As a result, the terror of the Lord fell on the people, and they went out united" (v. 7). In another indication of internal change wrought by the Spirit, Saul gave credit to God for the victory the people of Israel had won. The movement of the Spirit brought Saul to declare publicly where the glory belonged. "Today the Lord has provided deliverance in Israel" (v. 13). Saul's royal ministry began on a very good note! Sadly, however, it did not stay that way.

The fourth and perhaps most intriguing theological component of the work of the Spirit in the anointing of King Saul was Samuel's assurance that, following the signs of the Spirit's presence, "God is with you" (10:7). The king should do what the Lord placed upon his heart because the Lord would be present with him, enabling him to accomplish his work. This does not mean that everything Saul did was from God. It does indicate that Samuel believed Saul would be led by the Lord, at least in the first instance, to do God's will. And soon after, we are told, "God changed his heart" (v. 9).

From a pneumatologic perspective, 1 Samuel 10 is striking because Samuel's prophecy and its fulfillment indicate a tight relationship between the activity of the "Spirit" (v. 6) and the activity of "God" (v. 9). According to Old Testament scholar Daniel Block, the relationship might be expressed as one of divine agency. Generally, in the Historical Books, the Spirit is God's agent of providence, of conveyance, of empowerment, and of prophetic inspiration.[7] It is also striking that the presence of the "Spirit" (v. 6) is tightly related to the presence of "God" (v. 7). The text intimately relates the Spirit to God when speaking of his activity and of his presence. *These two correlations—the identification of the Spirit's activity with God's activity and the identification of the Spirit's presence with God's presence—subtly, if inexorably, indicate that the author of 1 Samuel believed in the essential unity of the Spirit with God.* We shall see that the biblical canon develops these correlations progressively.

The Spirit Is Sovereign

Returning to the human side of the narrative, note that the successful outward aspects of Saul's kingship continued. However, there were spiritual defeats occurring at the same time. Chapters 13–15 recount three episodes where Saul was characterized outwardly by foolish acts and inwardly by self-centered motives. His authoritarian grasping for power resulted ultimately in his disobedience to God. A human being's internal disposition will determine his outward actions toward both God and humanity. God, as we shall see, is said to look into our hearts and to judge our actions.

Samuel, in his last great speech to Israel, warned both the nation and its king that they were subject to judgment. The king and the people were going to be judged if they did not turn their hearts entirely toward God and avoid doing evil (12:24–25). For many today, weighing the sovereign work of God in the life of his people alongside their personal responsibility raises the thorny philosophical

---

[7] The correlations between God's actions and the Spirit's actions are summarized in Daniel I. Block, "Empowered by the Spirit of God: The Holy Spirit in the Historiographical Books of the Old Testament," *Southern Baptist Journal of Theology* 1, no. 1 (1997): 44–45.

question of human free will versus divine predestination. While the Spirit of God definitely works sovereignly in the lives of people, the shape of his internal working should not be misconstrued. There is a complexity of movement between divine action and human response that is not easily defined in either a libertarian or a deterministic fashion. God moves with utter sovereignty even as he calls his people to act responsibly.[8]

Saul's Foolish Heart. The Lord, by his Spirit, worked in the heart of Saul and used him powerfully and often successfully to wage war against Israel's enemies (14:47–48). However, Saul's heart did not lead him to respond properly to all of the Lord's commands. At the beginning of his kingship, Saul was consecrated with oil and given the command to wait upon the Lord, who would guide him through the priest Samuel (10:8). However, Saul demonstrated on at least three occasions that his heart was not properly responsive to the Spirit of God speaking through the voice of Samuel.

First, when the Israelite army was hard-pressed at Gilgal, and Samuel had not yet appeared, Saul took the authority to make ritual sacrifice into his own hands (13:7–9). Saul cloaked his power grab in pious language, but Samuel was clearly unimpressed. "You have been foolish. You have not kept the command the LORD your God gave you" (13:13). Saul's disobedient grasping after authority could not be excused as a religious act. The priest Samuel reminded King Saul that the sovereign God can see into human hearts (13:14). Due to his evil heart and actions, God now rejected Saul's kingship as a lasting institution.

---

[8] While I remain personally uncommitted, Kenneth Keathley offers a compelling philosophical theology that mediates between the Christian alternatives of Calvinism and Arminianism. Kenneth Keathley, *Sovereignty and Salvation: A Molinist Approach* (Nashville: B&H Academic, 2010).

On a second occasion, at Beth-aven, Saul's foolishness endangered the life of Israel's best warrior, his own son Jonathan. Confusing the Lord's vengeance with his own, Saul placed his troops under an oath to not eat until that evening (14:24). Jonathan was out working and winning battles while Saul was making this rash and self-centered oath. Ignorant of the king's oath, Jonathan ate some honey to refresh himself before going back into battle. The subsequent discovery ceremony identified Jonathan as a culprit for disobeying Saul, but the people saved the valiant son in spite of the foolish father's abuse of authority (14:45). During this second event, Saul again demonstrated an undue sense of authority over the priesthood (14:19).[9]

On a third occasion, Samuel told Saul that God wanted the Amalekites to be completely destroyed (15:3). The Lord had earlier instituted the harsh practice of *cherem* for special moral cases in the pagan nations closest to Israel. During the period of the conquest, wicked peoples within Israel's borders were to be utterly wiped out, explicitly so they would not lead the Israelites to engage in idolatry (Deut 25:19). Alas, Saul decided that the finer spoils from the Israelite victory over the Amalekites were not worthy of "devotion" to the Lord.[10] The more valuable people, animals, and things were therefore preserved, in spite of the Lord's explicit command through Samuel (1 Sam 15:9). After reminding him of his ordination, Samuel

---

[9] Saul "treats both the divine object and the divine method rather carelessly. Instead of inquiring of the priest, Saul commands him to do specific things, which are primarily under the authority of the priesthood." Tsumura, *The First Book of Samuel*, 366.

[10] *Cherem* means "devotion," indicating that the pagan peoples in Israel were intended by God for complete destruction. For a careful discussion of the relationship between God's moral judgment on the Canaanites and the blessing God intended for all nations, see Christopher J. H. Wright, *Old Testament Ethics and the People of God* (Downers Grove, IL: IVP Academic, 2004), 472–80.

confronted Saul with a poignant couple of questions, "So why didn't you obey the LORD? Why did you rush on the plunder and do what was evil in the LORD's sight?" (15:17–19). Samuel remembered that the Spirit had rushed upon Saul to anoint him (11:6). But rather than turning his own heart toward the Lord, Saul greedily rushed upon the spoils (15:19).

Saul made several excuses for not utterly destroying the Amalekites and their possessions. Perhaps the most cynical and sacrilegious reason he gave was that he wanted to make a sacrifice to the Lord with the spoils (15:21). But Samuel would brook no such deviation of religious practice into spiritual hypocrisy. "Does the LORD take pleasure in burnt offerings and sacrifices as much as in obeying the LORD? Look: to obey is better than sacrifice, to pay attention is better than the fat of rams" (v. 22). The Lord then declared his judgment on the first king of Israel: "Because you have rejected the word of the LORD, he has rejected you as king" (v. 23). These are devastating words, and Saul understood their import, to a limited extent.

Saul soon came back to Samuel to admit he had committed wrong. But this confession should not be confused with genuine repentance, for Saul was not really bothered by his sin against the Lord. The king was more concerned with how things might look before the people (15:30). Saul's heart was far from the Lord even as his ceremonialism before the people told a different story. However, the Lord knew Saul's heart beneath the religious charade, just as he knows our hearts when they go astray yet seek to hide themselves from view.

In chapter 16, the Lord chided Samuel, who continued to mourn over the foolishness of his protégé, Saul. In spite of Samuel's personal feelings to the contrary, God decided the time for choosing a new leader was at hand. Samuel was then sent to the house of Jesse, a descendant of Boaz and Ruth, of the tribe of Judah. He was instructed to wait as the Lord identified one of Jesse's sons as the future king. While Samuel was impressed with the stature of some of the brothers, the Lord was not. After all, Saul had impressive stature before men, but a wicked heart before God. "Humans do not see what the LORD sees, for humans see what is visible, but the LORD sees the heart" (16:7). God made his choice of the next king on the basis of the Spirit's probing of the human heart.

The Spirit Comes and the Spirit Leaves. When David, the least of the sons of Jesse, appeared from the field, the Lord informed Samuel that this handsome youth would be the new king. After Saul had been rejected and David had been anointed, two profoundly spiritual events occurred. The first happened in David's life. The second occurred in Saul's life. The Spirit came upon one. The Spirit left the other. The Spirit of God moves with sovereignty and freedom.

First, after Samuel had anointed David with oil, "the Spirit came powerfully on David from that day forward" (16:13). The powerful coming of the Spirit upon the second king was like that upon the first king, but the duration of his stay was different. The Spirit came to David "from that day forward." Theologically, this statement should not be seen as an indication that David was born again at that moment (as in John 3), for the Spirit's personal work of regeneration and justification awaited the coming of the Son of God, David's own future descendant, in the flesh first (John 16:7; Rom 1:2–4). Nor is this statement a guarantee that the Spirit would never depart from David, as Psalm 51 indicates the Spirit could at least potentially depart from the second king. Rather, 1 Samuel 16:13 contains a simple statement regarding the Spirit's continuing presence with David. Likely, it indicates that the Spirit would continue to empower David in his office as king. Its significance is also found in the negative relief cast upon Saul, whom the Spirit left, in comparison with the presence of the Spirit in David's life.

The second profoundly spiritual event, then, occurred with Saul. "Now the Spirit of the LORD had left Saul, and an evil spirit sent from the LORD began to torment him" (1 Sam 16:14). The gravity of the departure of the Spirit of the Lord cannot be overstated. God literally turned his back on his own anointed king. While Saul still ruled visibly for some time after this, God gave Saul over to his own passions and fears. This conclusion is reinforced by the fact that, not only did the Spirit of the Lord depart from Saul, but "an evil spirit sent from the LORD began to torment him."

What was the "evil spirit sent from the LORD"? Two major interpretations have been put forward. The first and more common view interprets *ruah-ra'ah* as an "evil spirit," a fallen angel. If this is the proper translation, then it is instructive that the evil spirit remained under the sovereign control of the Lord. While the fallen angel was responsible for his evil nature and acts, the Lord still used him to fulfill God's will. The interaction of the Lord with evil spirits and his continuing sovereignty over these rebellious beings is also seen in the early chapters of the ancient book of Job.

A second viewpoint argues that the evil spirit was not spiritually evil in origin but that the spirit worked bad effects upon Saul. According to the second interpretation, the better translation would be that *ruah-ra'ah* was "a spirit of disaster." This spirit was not necessarily personally evil. This spirit came from the Lord not to bring Saul into sin but to bring Saul to recognize the negative consequences of his foolish heart and his sinful actions.[11]

Whether *ruah-ra'ah* is interpreted as "evil spirit" or "spirit of disaster," this text still teaches that there was not just abandonment by the Spirit of the Lord but a negative judgment upon Saul. This judgment resulted in Saul being filled with terror. God was thus

---

[11] Tsumura, *The First Book of Samuel*, 427.

clearly saying no to Saul's kingship, and simultaneously preparing to say yes to "a man after [God's] own heart" (13:14). Saul's courtiers suggested that whenever Saul was tormented, a musician under retainer should play his lyre and sing to Saul.

In a poignant twist, that musician was none other than the new king himself, David (16:15–23). The narrative of 1 Samuel 16 poetically and powerfully reminds us that the Spirit of God is sovereign. The Spirit retains free authority, even over kings whom he previously empowered to serve in an office. The gifts of God may not be presumed upon by anyone. God may empower one king, disempower that king, and raise up another king in his place. He may even allow the incoming king to serve for a time in the first king's own palace. The Spirit of God remains sovereign, no matter what human sovereigns desire. The Spirit, in his divine freedom, may bring down one person and lift up another, for the Spirit remains divinely sovereign.

The Spirit Is the Lord

While the narrative of the books of Samuel is fascinating, the theological implications of certain linguistic choices should not be missed. The author made a particularly subtle but theologically significant literary move in chapters 18 and 19. His use of a summary formula in 18:12—"the LORD was with . . . but had left . . ."—does more than rehearse the description of the Spirit's movement in chapter 16. In chapter 16, we are told that with David's anointing, "the Spirit of the LORD came powerfully on David" (v. 13). A little later, we are also told, "Now the Spirit of the LORD had left Saul" (v. 14). In chapter 18, the description of these two events is shortened and historicized with, "the LORD was with David but had left Saul." This short description contains what has been called "a kind of *Leitmotiv* running through the stories of David and Saul."[12] "The Spirit," we may note, is herein identified as "the LORD."

After the Spirit came upon David and abandoned Saul, it became publicly obvious that there had occurred a shift in charismatic authority. Saul remained king, but David was the one who was now blessed with success after success. The women who sang of Israel's victories ascribed thousands to Saul, but tens of thousands to David (16:7). Saul's own daughter, Michal, fell in love with David and protected him from her father (18:20; 19:11–17). Saul's own son Jonathan recognized the transfer, too, and tried to defend David from his mercurial and jealous father (19:1–6). With every reminder of David's blessing, Saul sank deeper into an irrational rage.

The narrator's repeated means of describing David's divine authorization encapsulated the success-ridden presence of God in his life: "the LORD was with him." This formula appears thrice in chapter 18 alone (vv. 12, 14, 28) and at numerous other points in the Saul–David cycle (cf. 1 Sam 16:18; 17:37; 2 Sam 5:10). For the purpose of discovering the identity of the Holy Spirit, it is noteworthy that the author of the narrative used "the LORD" as a substitute of equivalency for "the Spirit of the LORD."

While in 16:13 "the Spirit" came powerfully upon and remained with David, in subsequent references, the author simply states that it was "the LORD" who was with David. In other words, from 16:18 on, "the Spirit" who had remained with David since his anointing is now referred to directly as "the LORD." The first part of the formula of 18:12 brings together the coming of the Spirit upon David in 16:13 with the continuance of the Lord with David in 16:18 and following: "The LORD was with David." Whether the name "Spirit"

---

[12] P. Kyle McCarter Jr., *1 Samuel: A New Translation with Introduction, Notes and Commentary*, Anchor Yale Bible Commentary (Garden City, NY: Doubleday, 1980), 281. Cf. p. 30.

or the name "LORD" is used, we are doubtlessly dealing with the same subject.

The second part of the formula of 18:12 adds that the Lord "had left Saul." The verb used in 18:13 is the same verb used in the earlier spiritual report about Saul after David's anointing. Both 16:14 and 18:12 speak of God as having *kur*, "left" or "departed," Saul. In the first case, it was *Ruah-Yahweh*, "the Spirit of the LORD," who departed from Saul. In the second case, it was *Yahweh*, "the LORD" who departed from Saul. Thus, in a second instance, for the author of the books of Samuel, "the Spirit of the LORD" is "the LORD."

Theologically, we are driven to note both the unity and the difference. There is both a distinction between *Ruah* and *Yahweh* and an identification between *Ruah* and *Yahweh*. The Spirit *is with* the Lord, and the Spirit *is* the Lord. The *Ruah* is with *Yahweh*, and the *Ruah* is *Yahweh*. This dialectic, this alternation of distinction and identity, between God and his Spirit helps create an intertextual "echo" that will be heard again and again into the New Testament.

The "evil spirit sent from God" also continues to make his appearance in the life of Saul, tormenting him, even to the point where Saul tried to pin David against a wall with a javelin, more than once (18:10–11; 19:9–10). After the second failed assassination effort, David fled the palace with assistance from Michal, Saul's daughter. The enraged king, not for the last time, sent troops after David, to kill him. But the Spirit was still acting on David's behalf, even when Saul was trying to murder David. This was repeatedly demonstrated at Ramah, where the Spirit of God came positively upon three groups of Saul's agents, prompting them to prophesy the word of the Lord and forsake trying to kill David (19:19–21).

Finally, when Saul himself personally went after David at Ramah, where the latter had fled to be with Samuel, the Spirit also came again upon Saul. Saul was so positively overwhelmed by the return of the Spirit of the Lord in his life that he entered Ramah prophesying and continued prophesying before Samuel, even stripping himself of his royal finery (19:23–24). The Lord remained in control of Saul's life, blessing him with his presence when he deemed it good and terrorizing him with the "evil spirit" when the Lord deemed that necessary. In each case, the Spirit of God applied the sovereign will of God.

Summary

From the Saul–David narratives, which extend from 1 Samuel 10 through 1 Samuel 19, we have learned three significant truths about the identity of the Spirit of God: First, we learned in chapters 10 and 11 that the Spirit is personally correlated with "God." To speak of the Spirit is to speak of deity. Second, we learned in chapter 16 that the Spirit exercises divine sovereignty. The Spirit determines whom he will use and whom he will not use. When thinking of the Spirit, we must think of him as acting freely in a way that only God may act. Third, we learned in chapters 18 and 19 that the Spirit is personally identifiable with "the LORD" as well as with "God." The Spirit of God is thereby explicitly identified as the covenant deity of Israel.

Those who think of the Spirit of God in impersonal terms should be shaken with the implications of this personal identity between the Spirit and God. The Spirit is not a mere "force" or "power," as some contemporary mythologies proclaim. The Spirit of God is not subject to human whim and will, as if he could be commanded to do what we wish. The Spirit is the God who continues to guide all his creatures to do what he freely wills. The Spirit is also the covenant Lord over Israel, who freely deals with those who live in covenant with him, no matter what their place among the people happens to be. The sovereign Spirit, who is the Lord God, remains in charge.

From firmly establishing the important truth regarding the identity of the Spirit with respect to God—that the Spirit is himself the sovereign Lord God—we may now turn to a consideration of who the Spirit is with respect to who humanity is and what humanity must become.

CHAPTER 3

Why Call the Spirit "Holy"?
Insights from Psalm 51

There are only three occasions in which the Old Testament refers to the Spirit of God as "the Holy Spirit." The paucity of Old Testament references is striking, because the New Testament uses the title so very often. A progress in revelation about God within Scripture should not surprise us, for God works to bring people, both individually and as a community, from immaturity into full maturity in their relationship with him (Heb 5:11–14). Nevertheless, the Spirit most definitely is referred to as the "Holy Spirit" within the Old Testament. The first and most significant time this occurs is in David's psalm of confession, Psalm 51. The other two places occupy succeeding verses in the prophecy of Isaiah 63 (vv. 10–11). Isaiah uses "holy" in reference to the Spirit as a way of providing a contrast to the rebelliousness of Israel, while David uses "holy" to indicate God's pure otherness. We focus here upon Psalm 51.

Dietrich Bonhoeffer referred to the book of Psalms as "the Prayerbook of the Bible." According to that twentieth-century Christian martyr, God gave us the psalms to show us how our hearts must be shaped through prayer to God. God grants us the various prayers that we require for the various occasions that arise in our lives. Bonhoeffer also noticed how Jesus fashioned the Lord's Prayer as a summative exercise, drawing all of the psalms together. Therefore, the psalms should be read and prayed as Jesus read and prayed them. "The psalms have been given to us precisely so that we can learn to pray them in the name of Jesus Christ."[1]

Bonhoeffer discovered ten different types of psalms, of which Psalm 51 is a prayer for dealing with guilt. He cited Martin Luther, who argued that the psalms must be read in an attitude of reflection, reverence, and petition, with the aid of the Holy Spirit: "[O]ne must be still and quickly reflect on the words of the Psalm; for they demand a quiet and restful soul, which can grasp and hold to that which the Holy Spirit there presents and offers."[2] All the psalms are intended to help us pray, but the particular purpose of the "penitential psalms" is to assist us in repenting of sin, so that the sinner may become holy. The psalms about guilt are intended to "lead us into the very depth of the recognition of sin before God."[3]

Guilt. In the discussion that follows, we shall examine the fifty-first psalm from the perspective of its confession about God, its confession about human sinfulness, and its petition for human transformation. Before delving into the three parts of the psalm, let us rehearse the historical background to it. Psalm 51 was written, like seventy-two of the other psalms, by David. The Israelite king's role in developing the book of Psalms prompted Charles Haddon

---

[1] "The Prayerbook of the Bible," in Dietrich Bonhoeffer, *Life Together and Prayerbook of the Bible*, ed. Geffrey B. Kelly, trans. Daniel W. Bloesch and James H. Burtness, Dietrich Bonhoeffer Works (Minneapolis: Fortress, 1996), 5:157.

[2] Martin Luther, foreword to the Psalms, in *Die Bibel oder die ganze Heilige Schrift des Alten und Neuen Testaments* (Luther's German translation of the Bible), cited in Bonhoeffer, *Life Together and Prayerbook of the Bible*, 161.

[3] Bonhoeffer, 171.

Spurgeon to tag it "The Treasury of David."[4] It certainly is a treasury of prayer, originally set to music, much of it authored by or on behalf of the second monarch of Israel. David's role in the writing of Psalm 51 came as a result of the most difficult crisis in his life, when he discovered how wretched a sinner he really was.

We saw in chapter 2 with Saul that even a king chosen and anointed by God could still be foolish and wicked in his heart, words, and deeds. But the problem of sin was not restricted to the son of Kish; it was also shared with the son of Jesse. Second Samuel 11 begins our tawdry tale. While kings traditionally went out to war, one spring, David decided he would spend time in his palace and send his lieutenants in his place (2 Sam 11:1). This self-centered action set the stage for the greatest sins committed by David in his otherwise exemplary life. The idolatry of the self is at the root of so much human sin.

One evening, while his troops were off at war, David got up from his bed to gaze out with leisure over the rooftops from his palace. There, his eyes fell upon a beautiful, bathing woman, who might perhaps be excused for thinking all the men were away at war. The responsible men were at work, but their irresponsible king was lounging luxuriously, preparing his heart for further sin. His thoughts and deeds, alas, would steadily progress from laziness to lustfulness to premeditated murder. The king sent for the bathing beauty, whose name was Bathsheba and his lustful heart led his willing body into full-fledged adultery. He then sent Bathsheba home, perhaps thinking nobody would ever know of his wicked deed. But she soon sent word back to the palace that she was expecting a child (vv. 2–5).

---

[4] See Charles H. Spurgeon, *The Treasury of David*, online at https://www.bible-studytools.com/commentaries/treasury-of-david/.

Moses had previously warned the tribes of Gad and Reuben about the temptation they would face if they did not join with the rest of the people when they went to war (Num 32:20–24). He spoke words that echo into David's life too: "Be sure your sin will find you out" (v. 23 ESV). David, however, believed, to the contrary, that his sin could be hidden. If David's first abuse of power was to excuse himself from work, and his second abuse of power was to set a stage for adultery, then his third abuse of power was to use state assets to engage in a cover-up. Those who are granted public power and responsibility, even the anointed of God, must remember that there is no such thing as a private sin. There is always One who knows, and he will confront you with your sin, even if others are afraid to confront you. There can be no real cover-up.

The rest of David's wicked deeds in this episode are well-known. He called for Uriah, Bathsheba's husband, to come home, hoping the man might sleep with his wife. Then, when Bathsheba's illegitimate baby was born, Uriah would believe it was his own, and nobody would ever know differently. What David had not counted on was that Uriah would be a man of pristine integrity. Following Moses rather than David, Uriah refused to rest at home while his colleagues were at war. He stayed at the king's palace and prepared to return to war. David even tried to ply him with alcohol to act irresponsibly, but Uriah remained true to his task. At this point, David could have turned back, confessed to Uriah, repented before God, and awaited his just deserts. But David thought he was better than Uriah and smarter than God. He was neither. David added murder to his crimes and a second cover-up, this time not of rape but of murder.

This man of God, the anointed of the Lord, the one gifted with the Spirit, committed despicable deeds, issued from a wicked heart. Adding transgression to transgression, heedlessly wrecking life after life, David involved Joab and Bathsheba in the counsels of his seedy, soul-sickening sins. Ultimately, Uriah was killed off, and Bathsheba simply moved in with David after her period of mourning for Uriah had ended (2 Sam 11:26–27). Nobody seemed to be any the wiser to David's wickedness. Nor would anyone dare to inquire, because David was ultimately in charge. The anointed of God was, to use a foolish modern idiom, "bulletproof."

Or was he?

In Psalm 51, David teaches us that the renewal of the sinful human person happens by

- confessing God,
- confessing human sin, and
- requesting personal transformation.

Confessing God

What David had forgotten was that the Lord God knows all things. He knows what we have done, and he knows what is in our wicked hearts. Demonstrating that "your sin will find you out" (Num 32:30 ESV), God sent Nathan, a prophet, to confront David with his sin. Nathan came to the palace and shared a sad story with the enthroned monarch: A poor man had a ewe lamb that he bought and nurtured like a daughter. She was all the poor man had, and he cared for her dearly. But a rich man, who had plenty of sheep, had a traveler to host. Not wanting to part with any of his own wealth, the rich man outrageously took the ewe lamb from the poor man for the meal (2 Sam 12:1–4).

Upon hearing about this tragic criminal case, David blurted out with all the self-righteous indignation he could muster, "As the LORD lives, the man who did this deserves to die!" In so doing, David unknowingly denounced his own sin and pronounced the sentence he himself deserved (vv. 5–6).

The next moment revealed everything, for the prophet was God's man more than the king's man. The prophet must speak God's Word, whatever the response of the abusive potentate might require from his own life. Nathan cried out boldly and pointedly, "You are the man!" (v. 7). Preachers and artists have tried to capture that moment with the image of the prophet's finger pointed accusingly at the king. One may imagine the shock on David's face at being exposed for what he really was: a lazy, leering, adulterous, lying, abusive, murderous rich man who had used his powers to take away both the only love and the very life of a poor, virtuous person. David was morally despicable and spiritually bankrupt. Uriah was the hero; David, the villain. The story of David's life might have ended there as another sad but true morality tale.

Judgment. The judgment of God was pronounced immediately. The Lord reminded David, first of all, "I anointed you king over Israel, and I rescued you from Saul." God then reminded David of all he had given to him: "I gave your master's house to you . . . and I gave you the house of Israel and Judah, and if that was not enough, I would have given you even more" (2 Sam 12:7–8). The measure of David's evil was not whether another king might have done what he had done or worse. No, the measure of righteousness remained the character of God himself (v. 9). As another prophet once told another king, both of whom David knew intimately, God's character does not change (1 Sam 15:29). The penalty for such a betrayal, of God's calling upon a man's life and of God's gracious saving of that same life, must be severe. The punishment must account for King David's wretched wickedness and utter hypocrisy. If Saul was judged for his evil heart and disobedience of God's commands, certainly David must be judged for his own evil heart and disobedience of God's commands.

And the judgment fit the heart of the crime. David's own heart had been perverted by a disdain for fidelity to family virtue. Thus, David's judgment would come through his family's infidelity, an infidelity they had learned from their father. "I am going to bring disaster on you from your own family" (2 Sam 12:11). The subsequent stories about Amnon's rape of his sister and of Absalom's rebellion against his father make for gruesome retelling (ch. 13–18).

Moreover, because David tried to keep his evil actions secret, God was going to make sure these despicable deeds were exposed to the whole nation (12:11–12). David could not expect to hide his sin behind a veil of hypocrisy while he claimed to be God's anointed. One simply does not pervert the justice of God, especially when one has been anointed to uphold that very justice. The righteous character of God demands both justice and a punishment to fit the crime. The crime, though committed against Uriah, was ultimately a crime against God himself. The Lord reminded David, "You despised the Lord's command by doing what I considered evil" (v. 9).

Justification. But divine judgment was not the final result of this greatest of moral crises in David's life. Amazingly, David did the only proper thing for a reprehensible sinner: he recognized and embraced the severest truth about himself without fanfare. Having his sins plainly disclosed to him brought him to say only one thing to Nathan, "I have sinned against the LORD" (v. 13). The words are few and simple, but sufficient to describe the movement in his heart. In Psalm 51, the moral simplicity of David's confession is provided with more detail, but the basics are the same. David could only confess that he had sinned against the Lord. The end result for David, therefore, was not separation from God, but a promise that his sins were removed from him and that he would not die (2 Sam 12:13).

The perceptive reader will remember that Saul, too, had confessed his sin, both against the Lord and against the Lord's prophet (1 Sam 15:24, 30). Yet Saul was not forgiven. What was the difference between the two men? Why was David forgiven, while Saul was not? Two answers jump from the text: First, Saul engaged in a long, drawn-out attempt to justify himself (1 Sam 15:12–25). He did not appeal to God for his justification. He tried to justify himself. David, on the other hand, did not try to justify himself. Second, there is the matter of the heart's confession about God. Saul was more concerned with how things might appear before the people than about how things ultimately appeared before God. David, to the contrary, was not concerned with social appearances. He was driven by one issue above all others. David was driven by a passion to be right with God once again.

If David was not looking to himself for the reason of his request for justification before God, what was the moral basis for his request to God for forgiveness? Saul had found all sorts of reasons to justify himself. Saul tried to blame the situation, tried to blame the people, and tried even to blame God's religious requirements, and he finally only admitted his sin with reluctance. Saul's confession, moreover, sought to appease the prophet for political reasons. David did not appeal to religion, to the people, or to the difficult situation in which he found himself. David, instead, appealed to the character of God.

The Perfections of God. Psalm 51 begins with a confession of who God is as the moral justification for David's request for forgiveness. "Be gracious to me, God, according to your faithful love, according to your abundant compassion" (v. 1). David's appeal for grace was not based on his own character, but on God's character. In particular, David referred to the divine attribute of *chesed*, "loving-kindness" (KJV) or *racham*, "compassion." Both terms may be and often are translated as "mercy." But the divine perfection of mercy is not the only perfection to which David appealed.

Later, David added the perfection of divine righteousness to the perfection of divine mercy. Throughout his struggle with himself, the divine character was the only reason David ever cited as to why God might possibly forgive him for his reprehensible sin. "You are right when you pass sentence; you are blameless when you judge" (Ps 51:4). There was no effort on David's part to put God in the dock, or to demand that God explain why David should suffer. Divine righteousness is the only possible reason one could argue for human justification. We could continue our discovery of various attributes that David emphasized, but the most significant divine attribute for our purposes is holiness: God's Spirit is holy. We will have more to say about the perfection of holiness momentarily.

David understood that he could appeal to nothing within himself. He had nothing within his character or his actions that might form the basis for an appeal. If there is to be any forgiveness for a human sinner, it must be by reason of God's own mercifulness, righteousness, and holiness. The perfect character of God, displayed in his attributes, is the only reason any person might expect pardon from God. True confession must begin with a confession of who God is, for God's character is the only possible basis for any hope of forgiveness from God.

Confessing Human Sin

Soon after David confessed God's perfections, he turned his attention to confessing his own sin. *The connection between the confession of God's character and the confession of human sin is fundamental to an understanding of the human problem.* We were created in God's image, so we are intended to reflect the perfections of his character, including his holiness (Gen 1:26–27; Lev 11:44; Matt 5:48; 1 Pet 1:16). Both the Old and the New Testaments emphasize that we are to be holy because God himself is holy. The human heart's embrace of sin, which eventually results in sinful actions, contradicts the call to be holy.

Systematic theologian James Leo Garrett has argued that the concept of sin has gone missing from our cultural discourse because we have separated sin from this theological basis. As a corrective, he put forward two necessary presuppositions regarding sin: The first says, "Sin presupposes that in God's nature and will there is an objective frame of reference definitive of sin." Another way to say this is that sin is sinful because sin is against God. Sin is not primarily about the wrong done to other human beings, though that is wrong. Sin is sin because the human being's character has contradicted the character of God himself. The second presupposition appeals to the holiness of God as the definitive divine attribute that has been contradicted by sin. "Sin presupposes the existence of God as a personal being, as the Holy One."[5]

The Holiness of God. Sin, then, is theologically wrong because it is a direct contradiction of the holiness of God. But what does it mean to say, "God is holy"? And what makes the concept of divine holiness so important? The Hebrew adjective translated literally as "holy" or substantively as "Holy One" is *qadosh*. Old Testament scholars believe this term derives from the idea of separation or exaltation. The first meaning of holiness is that which is unique and transcendent. God is "the Wholly Other."[6] The term *Holy* could even be used as a name for God himself.

---

[5] James Leo Garrett Jr., *Systematic Theology: Biblical, Historical, and Evangelical*, 2nd ed. (North Richland Hills, TX: BIBAL Press, 2000), 1:522.

[6] Garrett, 1:240.

Isaiah related another concept of what it means that God is holy when he relayed his famous temple vision. The angels cried out that God is "holy, holy, holy" (Isa 6:3). The prophet was deeply smitten by the realization that he and the people were "unclean" and, therefore, woefully "ruined" (v. 5). But God purified the prophet's uncleanness with a burning coal from the altar (vv. 6–7). Subsequently, the idea that "holy" primarily means moral purity became a New Testament theme (e.g. 1 Pet 1:15–16). In summary, "holy" was a synonym for deity as well as an indicator of divine transcendence and of moral purity. Such holiness was required of God's people.[7]

The Sinfulness of Humanity. Holiness is the opposite of sin in all its forms. But what is "sin"? By my count, sin is mentioned 15 times in Psalm 51. The words used for sin come from five major word groups, each of which carries its own connotations. First, *pesa'* is used 93 times in the Old Testament and twice in Psalm 51 (vv. 1, 3). It is often translated as "transgression" or "rebellion." It comes from the verb *pasa'*, which means "to step forward," implying an intentionality to sin. A related noun, *pasha'*, meaning "transgressor," is used once (v. 13). Garrett discovered three major rebellions against God by Israel, each of which was described with this term.[8]

Second, *chatta'ath* has been translated variously as "sin," "penalty," or "sin-offering." It is used 296 times in the Old Testament and twice in Psalm 51 (vv. 2, 3). The related verb *chata'*, "to miss," is used twice in the psalm (vv. 4, 7). The root idea behind "sin" here is that of "missing the mark," or, more colloquially, "going off the path." While it might be easy to see this term in the modern sense of a "mistake," the personal intentionality in the Hebrew is evident. The cognate noun, *chatta'*, "sinners," is also found in verse 13. The

---

[7] Garrett, 1: 244–45.

[8] The rebellions at Rephidim, Mount Sinai, and Kadesh-barnea. Garrett, 529.

noun *chet'* also exists in this word group and may be translated as "sin," "guilt," or "punishment."

Where David wrote, "In sin my mother conceived me" (v. 5), three meanings are possible: David's conception was a sinful act; or, David himself was guilty from conception; or, David's birth involved a penalty for sin. The second option is used by Reformed theologians to buttress a doctrine of original guilt. The third option, that David's mother travailed due to Eve's sin, is more likely since it derives from Gen 3:14. The interpretation of verse 5, however one decides to translate it, remains contested.[9]

Third, *'avon* has been translated as "perversity," "iniquity," or "guilt." It is used 230 times in the Old Testament and thrice in Psalm 51 (vv. 2, 5, 9). Coming from the verb *'avah*, meaning "twist" or "pervert," *'avon* emphasizes the guilt resulting from human sin.

The fourth term related to sin in Psalm 51 is *ra'*, a very common term used more than 650 times in the Old Testament. It has a range of meanings, from "evil" to "bad" to "sad," but its use in Psalm 51:4 seems to require the translation "evil."

Fifth and finally, *dam* is used 361 times in the Old Testament, and once in Psalm 51 (v. 14). *Dam* means "blood" or "bloodguilt," indicating that David was guilty of human slaughter.

The uses of these various words for sin range, therefore, from the inception to the consummation of personal moral evil. The uses of the various words related to personal moral evil stretch from the intention to sin (*pesha'*) and the moral character of sin as evil (*ra'*) to the guilt that results from sin (*'avon*) and the penalty that sin requires (*chatta'ath*) all the way to the ultimate price for sin in blood

---

[9] Cf. Nancy deClaissé-Walford, Rolf A. Jacobson, and Beth LaNeel Tanner, *The Book of Psalms*, The New International Commentary on the Old Testament (Grand Rapids: Eerdmans, 2014), 456.

(*dam*). What ties these various uses together is that they are committed by a human being in rebellion against the perfect holiness of God's character. They thus demand divine judgment, final judgment, death.

When a person engages in sin, that action is directed primarily, even exclusively, against God. This is why, in spite of his horrific wrongs against Bathsheba, Uriah, and the entire nation of Israel, David cried out to the Lord God, "Against you—you alone—I have sinned and done this evil in your sight" (Ps 51:4). "Is the psalmist not guilty of committing harm against humanity as well as committing harm against God? The obvious answer is 'yes.' And the words of the Psalm are addressed to God alone."[10] According to James Orr, we definitely commit wrongs against our fellow human beings, but sin is a personal and religious moral offense against God alone.[11] In the end, every human being must face God on his or her own and be judged. Because we sin against God alone, the only one who can possibly help us before the divine throne remains God alone.

The knowledge that only God could save David brought the sinner to the petition portion of his prayer. The first five verses of Psalm 51 emphasize David's personal confession about God and about his sin. The remainder of the psalm contains his petition, his request. The confessions about God and humanity precede the petitions for God to act on behalf of humanity. Confession must always precede petition. The petitions start as an outworking of confession. Petition may not proceed until confession is made. The confession, as noted earlier, was first about God, then about the human self. A proper confession—of God's perfections and of humanity's perversions—enables proper petitions.

---

[10] DeClaissé-Walford, Jacobson, and Tanner, 456.

[11] James Orr, *God's Image in Man and Its Defacement in the Light of Modern Denials* (Grand Rapids: Eerdmans, 1948), 213.

Four of David's heartfelt petitions concern *ruah*, referring both to God's Spirit and to the human spirit. As noted earlier, *ruah* may be used of either God or of humanity in the Old Testament. The largest concentrations of the term "spirit" in the Psalter occur in the 51st and 104th psalms, each of which uses the term four times. Psalm 104 is concerned with the relation of *ruah* to creation, while Psalm 51 is concerned with the relation of *ruah* to redemption. In this way, two of the major activities of God—creation and redemption—are related to the Spirit of God.

Within Psalm 51, three of the uses of *ruah* refer to the human being while one refers to the divine being. In the uses applied to humanity, each time it is qualified by a significant descriptor, and twice it is connected with the *leb*, or "heart." These usages tell us much about the human person made in God's image as well as about God. They thus must be carefully reviewed. David employed these terms to request only one thing from God for himself: personal transformation.

"A Steadfast Spirit." In the first instance of *ruah*, David prayed, "God, create a clean heart for me and renew a steadfast spirit within me" (Ps 51:10). The "spirit" here is put in parallel with the "heart." David began by asking God to work radically in his life. He used a powerfully evocative verb, *bara'*, which indicates a de novo act of creation and was first used in Gen 1:1. In other words, David was asking God not for a mere reforming of his heart but for a new creation. This means that rather than an impure heart, David would need a pure heart. His depravity required not merely heart surgery but a heart transplant. Through Nathan's prophecy, the king was now aware that his spirit was thoroughly perverted by sin.

Because his heart had been totally twisted by sin—evinced in his acts of adultery, murder, and cover-up—David knew his whole inner makeup required a radical reordering. David recognized he could not do this on his own, for sin characterized everything about him. The center of public justice for the nation of Israel had no righteousness in his own private life. Therefore, this moral hypocrite appealed to God to do what he as a human being could not do. David prayed, "Renew a right spirit within me." Using *hadesh*, a Piel imperative verb in Hebrew, David made a fervent request for God to graciously grant him something "new" rather than merely reforming the "old" within him. The old spirit had failed and must be rejected, gotten rid of, destroyed. Only a radical personal transformation would do, and only God can do what is required.

And the characteristic attribute of the new human spirit must be that of *nakon*. This Hebrew participle indicates an entirely new orientation towards wholeness and a spirit established on a proper moral foundation. The parallelism between "pure heart" and "established spirit" indicates David's desire that God would work in his life to create within him a new person. David's new spirit must be different from his old spirit in the quality of its moral direction and in its stability. Where he had been woefully off the mark and decidedly inconstant, he needed to become morally reordered, and solidly so. David begged God to take away his old immoral and variable spirit and provide him with a new morally directed and stable spirit.

"Your Holy Spirit." The second instance of *ruah* in Psalm 51 concerns God's *Ruah Qadesh*, his "Holy Spirit." In the next verse, David blurted out from deep within his soul, "Do not banish me from your presence or take your Holy Spirit from me" (v. 11). As future chapters will show, the coupling of the character of God as "holy" with the presence of God as "Spirit" will have significant ramifications for the rest of the biblical canon. And as mentioned previously in this chapter, the term "Holy" could be used as a divine name, just as the term "Spirit" could. A divine meaning could be attached either to "Holy" or to "Spirit," but bringing the terms

together created a very unique divine title, "Holy Spirit." This name will later become exclusively used with regard to the third person of the divine Trinity.

The emotive power of the verse depends on understanding the personal histories of both Saul and David as successive kings of Israel. David knew the Spirit of God had come on his predecessor at his anointing as king (1 Samuel 10). And David himself had received the Spirit of God at his own anointing as king. First Samuel 16:13–14 shows the Spirit departing Saul and coming upon David. The Spirit remained upon David, and David saw for himself the terrorizing personal effects of the departure of the Spirit of the Lord from Saul and the concomitant coming upon Saul of the evil spirit. Saul had had everything a person could physically desire in this world, but he'd possessed no joy whatsoever, because he lacked the comforting presence of the Lord.

David knew there was only one source of joy: the presence of God's Spirit in his personal life. He understood, moreover, that the Spirit was not guaranteed to remain upon him forever except by divine grace. This is why he cried out from the depth of his being to God, "Take not your Holy Spirit from me" (Ps 51:11 ESV). The Holy Spirit is not the possession of a human being under the power of a human being, but the presence of God under the power of God. The Holy Spirit is God himself, working upon the human spirit. The Holy Spirit is God come close to the human heart. The Holy Spirit is God's Spirit, and the presence of God to the human spirit. The Holy Spirit is present in a human life only by grace. The only possible thing David could want was God's Spirit in his heart. He desperately desired the Spirit, so he begged God to never take Him away.

The attachment of the title "Holy" to "Spirit" also aids in the development of the personal desire for holiness. It is as if David knew that sin and holiness do not mix. If the Spirit is holy, then

God is holy. And since God is holy, he demands holiness from his own people, communally and personally. David's only recourse in the face of sin was confession, repentance, and a plea for God's radical mercy. David needed an internal transformation of the heart. In short, he appealed for an undeserved salvation from sin on the basis of God's extraordinary grace, a grace in which God graciously gives something from himself. God's holiness must be given to the human being.

"A Willing Spirit." The presence of God would be a torment to David's spirit if David's heart was not transformed. David understood that he needed a new heart in order to enjoy the presence of God's Spirit in his life. That is why he asked for a new heart and a reordered spirit (v. 10) before asking God not to remove his Holy Spirit from his life (v. 11). David also understood that he could not have God's spirit continually in his life apart from the continual transforming work of God in his spirit. Therefore, in the very next verse, he requested, "Restore the joy of your salvation to me, and sustain me by giving me a willing spirit" (v. 12).

Some translators have opted to treat the *ruah* in verse 12, the third instance of *spirit* in the psalm, as divine rather than human. They then often translate the adjective *nedibah*, which literally means "noble," as "free" or "generous." If *ruah* here refers to God, that would be a most proper understanding. But if *ruah* here refers to a human, then the preferred translation, which has been the majority view in the modern period, has typically been "willing." This difficulty in translating *ruah nedibah* is a product of the intimacy that God places between himself and his human creature. The only way a human spirit can truly be free is if God gives a freedom to the human being that can only come from God himself. True human freedom is a spiritual gift from the God who is freedom.

The fact that the human being is created in the divine image (Gen 1:26) and receives his breath from the breath of God (Gen 2:7) means there is a necessary and inextricable intertwining of the human life with the divine life. God will be present by his Spirit to the human being either in judgment or in blessing. David asked for blessing, which necessitated a change in his spirit. There would be no joy and no freedom apart from a critical transformation in the human spirit, an act that only God himself can work within the human spirit.

"A Broken Spirit." From verse 14 on, David's psalm of purification turns from a petition of personal transformation to a petition for personal worship. "Save me from the guilt of bloodshed, God—God of my salvation—and my tongue will sing of your righteousness." All of Saul's religiosity in worship could not save Saul. Samuel had warned Saul that God was more interested in obedience than in sacrifice. David had learned from Saul's error (v. 16).

He thus prayed the fourth instance of *ruah* in this psalm, "The sacrifice pleasing to God is a broken spirit. You will not despise a broken and humbled heart, God" (v. 17). David knew he needed radical personal transformation in order to worship God correctly, so he asked God to break his spirit. The verb *shabar* can range in meaning from "break" to "shatter" to "maim." The grace of spiritual brokenness is clearly emphasized through its twofold literary application. The activity of breaking is applied once to the spirit and once to the heart.

If you will kindly allow my personal testimony, I can attest that such a prayer, when answered, will scar the human heart. I have had my own heart torn in two by God during a period of intense prayer and Bible study. It happened as God was rehearsing the tenor of my entire life. The questions he answered struck at the core of my self-identity: Who am I? What was done to me? What have I done?

Who owns my future? When God broke my heart, I had never felt such pain in my life. It was not a physical pain, though it certainly felt like it. It was not a psychological pain, though it also struck deep into the soul.

The breaking of one's heart is a form of spiritual surgery that can only be performed by God as an act of divine grace. It changes you. It humbles you. It reminds you in an unforgettable manner that you are God's and God's alone, and he alone will determine who you are and what you will do. But then, after the most excruciating part, when your heart has been shattered, the Lord gently puts you back together. The healing comes, but you may never be allowed to forget what he has done. You will never want that to happen again.

There is no true personal worship without the pain of personal transformation. Be careful when you pray for personal transformation in order to personally worship God correctly, for spiritual brokenness is required. God breaks the heart so that he might prepare it to be filled with his joyful presence. David's final petitions move from requests for personal transformation and personal worship to a request to allow David to instruct others in true worship, worship from the heart (vv. 18–19). Three distinct types of petition may, therefore, be found in Psalm 51, a petition for personal transformation, a petition for personal worship, and a petition for communal worship.

Summary

David's song of guilt began with confessions and ended with petitions. The anchor of the petition portion of Psalm 51 is a request that God change David so that he might know God with joy rather than under judgment. Its fulfillment requires the divine grace of personal transformation so that God's Spirit may continue to be present to

David's spirit. The king requests the Holy Spirit of God to work his sovereign grace of breaking his human spirit, remaking it to be God's alone. The Holy Spirit is the spirit who changes those he loves by breaking their hearts and coming to live in them. The brokenness is necessary because the sin must be removed from us, the heart must be radically renewed, and the spirit must be reordered so as to be brought in line with God. He is the Holy Spirit who requires holy human spirits, who themselves need a holiness that only he, the Spirit of Holiness, may give.

Dear reader, please consider your personal confession and your personal petition. First, do you understand how great the Lord God is? Unless you see that God is the source of all that is good and right and holy, of all that is perfect, you will not perceive anything else correctly. Unless you see the perfections of God, you will not perceive the depth and gravity of your failure and of your utter dependence upon God.

Second, do you really know how horrible of a person you truly are? In light of the perfections of God, do you recognize your debilitating imperfections? Read again the descriptions of sin in Psalm 51 and ask the Lord to show you the truth about your depravity and spiritual poverty.

Third, will you then call only upon God in faith and ask him to change you? Will you beg God to place his Holy Spirit in your life such that he will never leave you? Will you ask him to transform you in such a way that you could only refer to it as a life-altering surgery of your heart? Will you pray that God would give you a spirit that longs to do his will rather than your own? I pray and hope that the Spirit will give you a heart that willingly and fervently desires God's will alone.

CHAPTER 4

Who Is the Holy Spirit to Jesus?
Insights from the Gospel of Matthew

A s we transition to the New Testament witness regarding the Holy Spirit's identity, it is absolutely necessary to take into account the relationship of the Spirit to the primary subject of the New Testament, Jesus of Nazareth. Who is the Holy Spirit to Jesus? It has often been noted that the Spirit was active in every aspect of the life of Christ. Perhaps the best way to see this is to turn to one of the Gospels and examine how Jesus and one of his evangelists spoke of the Spirit. We will take up the rich pneumatology of John in the next chapter, so we here choose one of the other Gospels, and Matthew is as convenient as another. Biblical theologians understand that the Gospel of John presents a Christology "from above," that is, from the perspective of his deity first, but the Matthean narrative strategy differs.

The Gospel according to Matthew, like the other Synoptic Gospels, presents a Christology "from below," that is, from the perspective of our Lord's humanity first. While the Synoptics begin with the human Jesus, they then proceed to disclose Christ's deity. Christology and atonement are, doubtless, the primary focus of the Gospel of

Matthew, but there is a pneumatology evident too. In the following discussion, we shall glance periodically at the other Gospels, even as our gaze rests upon Matthew. The Gospel of Matthew presents the Holy Spirit as the One who conceived Jesus, who is the continuous companion of Christ (first in his baptismal commission and later throughout his ministry), and who shares in the Godhead with the Father and the Son.

The Gospel of Matthew includes several accounts of how the Holy Spirit was involved in the life of Jesus. Elsewhere, I have argued that, according to the Synoptic Gospels, of which Matthew is canonically first, the Spirit interacts with Jesus in the four major events of his incarnation, baptism, ministry, and resurrection.[1] Our concern in this book is not with the work but with the identity of the Holy Spirit, so we shall emphasize the Spirit's personhood. We are thus less interested in the Spirit's role in the history of Jesus than in the Spirit's identity vis-à-vis Jesus Christ. This distinct goal allows us to affirm four truths revealed about the identity of the Holy Spirit in the Gospel of Matthew:

- the Spirit is the Conceiver of Jesus,
- the Spirit is the Commissioner of Jesus,
- the Spirit is the Companion of Jesus, and
- the Spirit shares deity with Jesus.

The Spirit Is the Conceiver of Jesus

Matthew 1:18–21 relates Joseph's understanding of the conception of Jesus. When Joseph discovered that Mary was expecting a child,

---

[1] Yarnell, "The Person and Work of the Holy Spirit," 489 (see intro., n. 1). When considering the whole witness of the New Testament, we can add that the Spirit is also involved in the death and in the exaltation of Jesus Christ. Yarnell, 429.

he was probably broken in heart. He had not known his betrothed bride intimately, so he knew that Mary did not carry his child. However, because he was "a righteous man," Joseph decided to divorce her without fanfare, reducing both her personal shame and any social penalty, which could be severe. The Lord, in response, sent an angel to instruct Joseph about what had really happened. The angel and the narrator speak of the conception of Jesus as involving the Holy Spirit. The language is theologically instructive.

First, the narrator stated, Mary "was pregnant from the Holy Spirit" (v. 18). This sentence speaks euphemistically of the belly as a womb. The agent for the presence of a child in Mary's womb is described in the Greek as *ek pneumatos hagiou*. As a preposition of origin, *ek* might be translated with a causative sense, "by" or "because of," or with a derivative sense, "from" or "out of." Either way, the baby within Mary did not originate from a man but from the Holy Spirit. Later, in a second explanation, the angel tells Joseph, "because what has been conceived in her is from the Holy Spirit" (v. 20). The Greek text states, *to gar en autai gennethen ek pneumatos estin hagiou*. This text is provided so as to show the importance of the verb, *gennethen*, "conceived." *Gennao* in its basic form means a physical generation, and that is the sense to be maintained here. Moreover, both Mary and the child are treated with a passive verb, such that the Holy Spirit is, again, highlighted as the initiator in the conception. The human person within Mary's womb is a product whose origin is the Holy Spirit himself. There are no significant textual variants in the tradition of these two explanatory phrases to encourage a different meaning.[2]

---

[2] There is a variant in the earlier term in verse 18, *genesis*, with *gennasis* substituted in a few texts. The former word emphasizes the origin of the birth and the latter the birth process itself. The two explanations that follow this term reinforce the majority tradition's use of *genesis*, "origin." R. T. France, *The Gospel of Matthew*,

The physical generation of the human Jesus, on the basis of the relevant Gospel texts, may be located within Mary as originating, causally and/or derivatively, from the Holy Spirit of God. According to the creedal tradition, therefore, the humanity of Jesus was "born of the virgin Mary" (Apostles' Creed) or "born from the substance of his mother" (Athanasian Creed). The Nicene Creed more fully states that the Son of God "descended from heaven and took flesh by the Holy Spirit and the virgin Mary."[3] The generation of the human Jesus in the womb of Mary by the Spirit seems intended to guarantee that he would share in our humanity yet without our depravity.[4]

Alongside the Holy Spirit's generation of the human nature of the person Jesus Christ, the early church fathers properly spoke of the eternal generation of the divine nature of the Son from the Father. The most explicit affirmation of a twofold generation of Christ, eternally from the Father and temporally from the Spirit through Mary, occurs in the Formula of Chalcedon: Our Lord Jesus Christ was "as regards his Godhead, begotten of the Father before the ages, but yet as regards his manhood begotten [born], for us men and for our salvation, of Mary the Virgin."[5] The eternal begetting of the Son has generated (pardon the pun) great controversy among evangelicals in recent years.[6]

The New International Commentary on the New Testament (Grand Rapids, MI: Eerdmans, 2007), 46n14.

[3] All quotations of these three primary creeds in this book are from the new translations in the appendix of Malcolm B. Yarnell III, *God the Trinity: Biblical Portraits* (Nashville: B&H Academic, 2016), 239–43.

[4] Daniel L. Akin, "The Person of Christ," in Akin, *A Theology for the Church*, 432–33.

[5] All quotations of the Chalcedonian formula are from the Schaff translation available in Gregg R. Allison, *Historical Theology: An Introduction to Christian Doctrine* (Grand Rapids: Zondervan, 2011), 376–77.

[6] See, for example, Fred Sanders and Scott R. Swain, eds., *Retrieving Eternal Generation* (Grand Rapids: Zondervan, 2017).

What should not be a matter of controversy among evangelicals is that Matthew affirms the Holy Spirit's generation within Mary of the human nature of Jesus. The Holy Spirit is the Conceiver of the human Jesus Christ, who is also the eternal Son of God. The Spirit conceived his humanity, specifically so that he would "save his people from their sins" (1:21). Humanity's salvation through Christ Jesus required that he be conceived by the Holy Spirit in the womb of the Virgin.

Not only did the Spirit conceive the human Jesus. After conceiving Jesus in Mary, the Holy Spirit remained active as a personal companion to Jesus throughout his human life, and beyond into glory. In the Gospel of Matthew, the economic work of the Son and the Spirit, as well as that of the Father, are closely correlated. The early church fathers spoke of the work of the Trinity as indivisible. Each of the three persons is involved in all of the divine works. The way the Son and the Spirit work together in the life of Jesus, as recorded in the Gospels, demonstrates an unparalleled intimacy between the two persons that fits with the patristic claim of an indivisible Trinity. To the initiation of their interdependent working we now turn.

The Spirit Is the Commissioner of Jesus

Following his conception, the first indication of the Spirit's role in the life of Jesus comes with his baptism. John the Baptist had been immersing (i.e., "baptizing") people in the Jordan River for the purpose of demonstrating repentance. But according to the late Anglican cleric R. T. France, John's "preparatory and symbolic baptism will soon give way to an effective 'baptism.'"[7] The activity of John

---

[7] R.T. France, *The Gospel according to Matthew: An Introduction and Commentary*, Tyndale New Testament Commentaries (Grand Rapids: Eerdmans, 1985), 93.

and his disciples, while certainly important and necessary, is only preparatory to the critical change needed within sinners. As we saw with the anointed King David, God requires a radical internal transformation from even the best of his people. This cannot be carried out by anyone but God himself in the person of his Holy Spirit. And Jesus Christ, the Son of God, according to the New Testament, is the only One who may give the Spirit.

John the Baptist told his followers, "I baptize you with water for repentance, but the one who is coming after me is more powerful than I. I am not worthy to remove his sandals. He himself will baptize you with the Holy Spirit and fire. His winnowing shovel is in his hand, and he will clear his threshing floor and gather his wheat into the barn. But the chaff he will burn with fire that never goes out" (Matt 3:11–12). John was adamant that his own person and ministry were vastly inferior to the person and work of Jesus Christ, and the Holy Spirit is the key to Jesus's manifest superiority in power.

Personally, Jesus is "more powerful" than John. The power of his person is not, moreover, human but divine in origin. The Baptist alluded to this, according to the Gospel of John, when he said, "After me comes a man who ranks ahead of me, because he existed before me" (John 1:30). Luke's chronology reminds us that John was, as a human being, somewhat older than Jesus (Luke 1–2), yet John stated, "he existed before me." John also said he was unworthy even to lace up the footwear of the Lord Jesus. The preexistence of Christ before the incarnation is thus implied even as his preeminence in authority and precedence in status are explicated. But the most important aspect, for our study, is the relation of Jesus with the Holy Spirit and baptism. Three major issues arise with regard to the Spirit and baptism: baptism with the Holy Spirit; baptism with the Holy Spirit and fire; and Jesus's own baptismal commission to a threefold office.

Baptism with the Holy Spirit. Several questions arise about the Spirit from this passage. First, what did John the Baptist mean that Jesus "will baptize you with the Holy Spirit"? Baptism here indicates an act of inundation or complete flooding. John spoke not of a particular ecclesiastical or personal action, ritual or experiential, but of the total immersion of a human life within the Spirit of God. Nor do the Gospel accounts of John's description specify a post-conversion experience. Of the seven New Testament references to baptism "in" or "with" the Holy Spirit, four recount John's promise (Matt 3:11; Mark 1:8; Luke 3:16; John 1:33), one recounts Jesus's own promise that he would soon baptize with the Holy Spirit (Acts 1:5), and one is Peter's memory that the promise was already fulfilled at Pentecost (Acts 11:15–17). Similarly, Paul taught that the church in its entirety had already been "baptized into one body" (1 Cor 12:13). "Baptism with the Spirit" apparently refers, in the first place, to the seminal event of the coming of the Spirit upon the whole church at Pentecost.

In Christian history, there have been a variety of attempts by equally fervent believers to correlate the passages regarding baptism with the Spirit, the gift of the Spirit, the filling of the Spirit, and the manifestations of the Spirit's presence. The weight of the biblical evidence indicates that baptism with the Holy Spirit is for the entire church, which receives the blessing of life in Christ originally at Pentecost. For theologians like me, who are influenced by Reformation theological exegesis, the baptism with the Spirit is a communal event. However, it may be inferred that baptism with the Spirit occurs for individuals subsequently during their evangelical conversion, since it is at the time of conversion that many contemporary evangelicals believe they receive the Spirit and are incorporated into the body of Christ.[8] Reformation-oriented theologians person-ally differ with their charismatic-oriented colleagues, who often de-scribe Spirit baptism as a post-conversion event. Whichever position is taken, it remains important for all orthodox Christians to affirm that life with the Trinity—the one God who is Father, Son, and Holy Spirit—remains necessarily an indivisible event.

Baptism with the Holy Spirit and Fire. A second important question arises regarding what John the Baptist meant when he said that Jesus will baptize "with the Holy Spirit and fire." Much can be learned by referring back to the prophets, of whom John the Bap-tist was the last and the greatest (Matt 11:9–11; 14:5). Isaiah, for instance, spoke of the Spirit as "a spirit of judgment and a spir-it of burning." His treatment of the spirit in this case emphasizes that the Spirit of God will purify God's people from their "filth" and "bloodguilt" (Isa 4:4). Such purification comes from a fire that will consume some while it cleanses others: "I will turn my hand against you and will burn away your dross completely; I will remove all your impurities" (Isa 1:25). Rustin Umstattd has demonstrated, against modern sensibilities to the contrary, that the biblical doctrine of the Spirit requires us to affirm that the Holy Spirit is the One who applies the judgment of God.[9]

According to John the Baptist, the Lord also will force open the difference between the wheat and the chaff. The baptism that Christ brings, with the Spirit and fire, is not intended for everyone in the same way. A separation between two categories of recipient will be made, idiomatically, on the Lord's "threshing floor," where a farming tool was used to throw the wheat into the air. The lighter chaff was separated by the wind as the heavier wheat fell. According

---

[8] Cf. Yarnell, "The Person and Work of the Holy Spirit," 491–93.

[9] Rustin Umstattd, *The Spirit and the Lake of Fire: Pneumatology and Judgment* (Eugene, OR: Wipf and Stock, 2017).

to John, the chaff, or unbelievers, will be thrown into a "fire that will never go out," while the Lord will "gather his wheat into the barn." This separation informs us that judgment—either temporarily in this life through purification or permanently in eternity through condemnation—is not the only activity of the Holy Spirit that Jesus brings to us in baptism.

The same Spirit who will bring a purifying judgment of redemption to the one and a final judgment of punishment to the other also brings blessing. The prophet Isaiah earlier said that when "the Spirit from on high is poured out on us," "the desert will become an orchard and the orchard will seem like a forest" (Isa 32:15). Later, he again used an agricultural metaphor to describe God's blessings by his Spirit: "For I will pour water on the thirsty land and streams on the dry ground; I will pour out my Spirit on your descendants and my blessing on your offspring" (Isa 44:3). Yes, the Son of God gives the Holy Spirit to bring judgment, but he also gives the Holy Spirit so that the people who are his may be blessed and blessed abundantly.

Commissioned to a Threefold Office. Soon after John made his pronouncement about Jesus's superiority, the Lord came to John to receive baptism. When John saw him, he hesitated to baptize Jesus due to the latter's greater status and greater baptism. However, Jesus said he needed to be baptized "to fulfill all righteousness" (Matt 3:15). This statement carries a threefold allusion related to the past, present, and future. First, Jesus referred back in time to the prophecy of the Suffering Servant. Second, he referred to the contemporary message of John, which his hearers would themselves know. Third, he referred ahead in time to the righteousness Christ himself would accomplish on behalf of the people through his cross (Isa 53:11; Matt 21:32; 27:19).

Jesus referred back to Isaiah's prophecy of the Suffering Servant, thereby granting insight into the role of the Spirit in the life of the Messiah. After his own water baptism, while coming up from the immersion, Jesus "saw the Spirit of God descending like a dove and coming down on him" (Matt 3:16). At the same time, "a voice from heaven said, 'This is my beloved Son, with whom I am well-pleased'" (v. 17). The prophecies of Isaiah had foretold the commissioning of Jesus at his baptism for his multivalent role as Messiah. Isaiah 42:1 (along with Ps 2:7) provided the basis for the baptismal commission of Jesus. Note particularly the references to his election as servant, as the one who works righteousness, and as the recipient of the Spirit from God: "This is my servant, I strengthen him, this is my chosen one; I delight in him. I have put my Spirit on him; he will bring justice to the nations." Isaiah 42:1–4 is later cited in Matt 12:18–21 as a means of summarizing Jesus's powerful ministry.

Why is the Spirit being given to the Son in fulfillment of the messianic promise of Isa 42:1? Three other prophecies of Isaiah, from chapters 11, 53, and 62, inform us of the purpose behind the coming of the Spirit upon the Messiah. All three of these other Isaian prophecies find fulfillment in the description of Jesus's baptismal commission, and they form echoes elsewhere in the Gospel of Matthew. In short, the Spirit of God comes upon the Messiah of God to empower Jesus for his threefold ministry as prophet, priest, and king.

First, referring to kingship, Isa 11:2 says that "the Spirit of the LORD will rest on" the Messiah. The idea here is that, unlike Saul, upon whom the Spirit came and departed, and unlike David, who would only retain the Spirit by grace, the Messiah would have the continual presence of the Spirit. The Spirit will "rest" upon the Messiah. Israel had seen king after king, all of whom were anointed, abuse their royal office and lose the Spirit's blessing upon them and their people. But Isaiah looked forward to a time when the palace might be empty and the Spirit would rest upon all the people (Isa 32:14–15).[10] Why would the Spirit first come to rest on the Messiah? Because the Spirit requires the Messiah to exercise the rule of God, even as the Messiah gives the Spirit to all the people of God. The Spirit that rests upon the Messiah has a sixfold ministry with the Messiah to grant him wisdom to rule. He is a "Spirit of wisdom and understanding, a Spirit of counsel and strength, a Spirit of knowledge and of the fear of the Lord" (11:2).

However, the coming of the Spirit upon all the people, human leaders included, still requires the Spirit to remain upon the perfect king, the long-awaited Messiah, for a prophetic purpose. A second prophecy regarding the coming of the Spirit, this time with regard to his prophetic office, upon the Messiah thus begins in Isa 61:1. "The Spirit of the Lord GOD is on me, because the LORD has anointed me to bring good news." The Spirit, according to this prophecy, rests upon the Messiah in a way he rested upon no other. The Messiah will be "anointed" like other kings, but his role is different. It is primarily to preach the "good news," the gospel. Jesus read this same text near the beginning of his ministry as a way of publicly informing his own synagogue of the fulfillment of Isaiah's messianic prophecies in himself (Isa 61:1–2; Luke 4:18–19). The Spirit rests upon the Messiah to empower him for authoritative proclamation as the great Prophet of God.

---

[10] "Yet the Davidic kings had come to manifest a spirit which had little of God in it. Craven, cynical, pompous, they seemed to be spiritually bankrupt, so much so that Isaiah was led to testify that the palace was empty (32:14) and envisioned a day when the Spirit of God would be visited on the people as whole (32:15) through their leaders." John N. Oswalt, *The Book of Isaiah Chapters 1–39*, The New International Commentary on the Old Testament (Grand Rapids: Eerdmans, 1986), 279.

So far, we have seen that Isaiah prophesied a kingly ministry for the Messiah (Isa 11) and a prophetic ministry for the Messiah (Isa 62). The third ministry for which the Spirit was prophesied to equip the Messiah is that of a priest making the atoning sacrifice. As already noted with Isaiah 42, the Spirit will come upon the Messiah, in the end, so that "he will bring justice to the nations" (v. 1). The prophecies of the Suffering Servant that begin with Isaiah 42:1 build toward the climactic description of the atoning death and resurrection of the messianic servant, which starts with Isa 52:13.[11] Toward the end of that climactic prophecy, we are reminded of the Messiah: "my righteous servant will justify [make righteous] many, and he will carry their iniquities" (Isa 53:11).

The penal substitutionary nature of the final servant song in Isa 52:13–53:12 is well-known, as is the prophetic foresight of the passage's fulfillment in the life, death, and resurrection of Jesus. The Suffering Servant as Messiah, therefore, is also the Priest who offers himself as the effective sacrifice for the sins of God's people. This is ultimately why Jesus, the messianic Priest empowered by the Spirit, said that he would in baptism symbolically "fulfill all righteousness" (Matt 3:15). At his water baptism, Jesus Christ, the eternal Son of God become man, was commissioned by the Father and empowered by the Holy Spirit to fulfill his unique messianic office as the universal prophet, priest, and king. The Spirit of God was the executive instrument of the Father in the commissioning to a threefold ministry of the Son at his water baptism.

---

[11] John N. Oswalt, *The Book of Isaiah Chapters 40–66*, The New International Commentary on the Old Testament (Grand Rapids: Eerdmans, 1998), 107–8.

The Spirit Is the Companion of Jesus

As we have just seen, the Gospel of Matthew interacts frequently and meaningfully with the book of Isaiah. But Matthew does not depend on Isaiah's prophecies alone. The critical apparatus for the United Bible Societies' Greek New Testament, which is fairly reserved on such matters, "lists fifty-four direct citations of the OT in Matthew and a further 262 'allusions and verbal parallels.'"[12] A common form of citation is the "formula-quotation," such as, "Now all this took place to fulfill what was spoken by the Lord through the prophet" (Matt 1:22). While the other evangelists certainly interact with the Old Testament, Matthew shows a sustained effort to weave prophecy into his thought process. "Among the gospels Matthew stands out for his sustained and creative presentation of this theme of fulfillment in Jesus."[13]

The Gospel according to Matthew refers to Hebrew Scripture in pneumatic ways too. These include a series of hermeneutical controversies as well as a running thematic incorporation of the experiences of David and Saul regarding the Holy Spirit and evil spirits. God's Spirit is presented as the companion both of Christ and of his followers in their discourses over biblical interpretation. The interlocutors for Christ and his disciples in biblical interpretation, during which the Holy Spirit is present to guide their spirits toward truth, include both Satan and unbelievers.

After his baptism, the next reported encounter of Jesus with another person was with "the tempter" in the wilderness (Matt 4:3). The Spirit is the one who directs Jesus during this encounter, and proper interpretation of Scripture is the form of their controversy.

---

[12] France, *The Gospel of Matthew*, 10.

[13] France, 11.

"Then Jesus was led up by the Spirit into the wilderness to be tempted by the devil" (4:1). As with the Saul–David narratives of 1 Samuel, the Holy Spirit and the evil spirit are placed in moral opposition to each other. Likewise, the sovereignty of the Holy Spirit is affirmed in that he is the one who coordinates the encounter. The physical battleground for the conflagration is the wilderness, but the spiritual battleground is the Old Testament. The context suggests parallels with the experiences of Moses and Elijah, when the Israelites failed. But Jesus, unlike Israel, prevailed through exercising his mind and heart in a careful exegesis of Deuteronomy 6–8. For Jesus, Scripture is more important than bread (Matt 4:4); one may never presume upon God (v. 7); and worship must be reserved exclusively for God (v. 10).

Matthew 4 pictures Jesus's ministry as shaped by a paradigm of activities: proclaiming the incoming kingdom of God (vv. 17, 23), calling his disciples to follow him (v. 19), performing various healings (v. 23), and casting out evil spirits (v. 24). Whereas Saul had no power over the evil spirit who terrorized him, and David feared the withdrawal of God's Spirit from him, Jesus cast out the evil spirits who terrorized people and continually retained God's Spirit without fear of withdrawal. Jesus also shared his companionship with the Holy Spirit and his power over evil spirits with his disciples. Jesus "drove out the spirits with a word" and brought healing (8:16). And he gave the disciples "authority over unclean spirits, to drive them out" and to bring healing (10:1). The human Jesus in word and deed is the fulcrum that determines on whom, from whom, and through whom the sovereign power of the divine Spirit concentrates, resides, and emanates.

"Blasphemy against the Holy Spirit." The difference between the Holy Spirit and evil spirits, and the proper relation of the former to Jesus Christ, cannot be overstressed. Jesus's teaching about the "blasphemy against the Holy Spirit" reinforces the importance of recognizing the divine Spirit's work in the life and ministry of Jesus Christ and the fundamental opposition of the Holy Spirit to evil spirits. Matthew began his report of Jesus's teaching on blasphemy with a recitation of the Messiah's endowment with the Spirit from Isa 42:1–4 (Matt 12:18–21). The emphasis seems to be on the gentleness of the Messiah as opposed to the death threats of the Pharisees (Matt 12:14). The profound power working through the gentle Messiah is the sovereign Spirit of God.

The Pharisees, deranged by their opposition to the ministry of Jesus, actually claimed that he cast out evil spirits "only by Beelzebul, the ruler of the demons" (v. 24). Jesus derided the ludicrous logic behind their claim, then proclaimed, "If I drive out demons by the Spirit of God, then the kingdom of God has come upon you" (v. 28). A little later, he argued that those who speak blasphemy, even against "the Son of Man," may be forgiven, but "the blasphemy against the Holy Spirit will not be forgiven" (v. 31). Again, "whoever speaks against the Holy Spirit, it will not be forgiven him, either in this age or in the one to come" (v. 32).

In its Matthean literary context, the unforgivable sin of blasphemy against the Holy Spirit occurs when somebody claims the work of God's Spirit is really the work of the evil spirit.[14] As if to drive home the irreconcilable opposition between that which is manifestly holy and that which is manifestly evil, the next three pericopes of Matthew 12 highlight the distinction between the evil and the good (evil and good trees, vv. 33–37; an evil generation, vv. 38–42; unclean and evil spirits, vv. 43–45). Those who misidentify the correlation between Jesus Christ and the Holy Spirit by stating that

---

[14] Blasphemy against the Spirit entails "a decisive choice of the wrong side in the battle between good and evil, between God and Satan." France, *The Gospel of Matthew*, 482–83.

Jesus has an evil spirit are subject to eternal damnation. This is why establishing the doctrine of the Holy Spirit as the companion of Christ remains so important.

The Human Spirit. As we have now seen, the Gospel of Matthew demonstrates that God is spiritual and that angels are spiritual too. However, human beings, who are made in God's image, are also spiritual beings. We are intended to be the companions of God through the created relation between our spirits and his Spirit (Gen 2:7). Perhaps recalling the garden of Eden, in the garden at Gethsemane, Jesus instructed the disciples to pray not to be tempted, because "the spirit is willing, but the flesh is weak" (Matt 26:41).

Jesus here indicated that the constituent makeup of the human being is at least mildly dualist, distinguishing "spirit" from "flesh." Moreover, the human spirit has limited power to wrestle with its passions, being opposed internally by the weakness of the flesh. Earlier, in his Sermon on the Mount, Jesus characterized the human spirit positively. He said the blessed human possesses humility, being "poor in spirit" (5:3).

Finally, with regard to a spirit-anthropology, Matthew follows the theology of Genesis in saying that the human spirit is withdrawn from the body at death. Jesus was fully human, and thus possessed a human spirit too. At the moment of his own death, "Jesus cried out again with a loud voice and gave up his spirit" (27:50). As fully human, Jesus had a human spirit; as fully divine, he is also Spirit and intimately related to the Holy Spirit.

Inspired by the Spirit. In a final lesson about the companionship between Jesus and the Spirit, we should see that the Lord taught his disciples about the spiritual basis of the Word of God. This was true both with regard to the existing Old Testament and in the New Testament, which for the disciples was forthcoming. He informed the Jews that the prophet David spoke as a result of being "inspired by the Spirit" (Matt 22:43). Through translating *en pneumati* as "by the Spirit," the Christian Standard Bible properly chose to emphasize the divine agency of the Spirit and the human instrumentality of David in the process of prophetic inspiration.

Jesus also told his disciples that they, too, would be inspired. Warning of coming persecutions, Jesus encouraged them not to worry about what to say. "For you will be given what to say at that hour, because it isn't you speaking, but the Spirit of your Father is speaking through you" (10:19–20). In this text, the Holy Spirit is invoked as the divine and inspiring presence in the life of the disciples. Peter, who plays a large role in the Gospel of Matthew, later similarly argued that the Holy Spirit had inspired the prophets and apostles to write their books (2 Pet 1:20–21; cf. 3:14–16).

The Spirit Shares Deity with Jesus

Matthew painted a complex portrait of the Holy Spirit in his relationship to Jesus Christ. The Holy Spirit conceived the man Jesus in the womb of the virgin Mary. The Holy Spirit commissioned Jesus to his ministry as prophet, priest, and king. The Holy Spirit is the continual companion of Jesus Christ, empowering his dominion over the evil spirits and inspiring his disciples. Matthew also pictures the close relationship between Jesus Christ and the Holy Spirit in its eternal dimensions. From the baptism of Jesus through the teaching of Jesus and into the giving of the Great Commission, Jesus presents the Holy Spirit as sharing fully in the deity of God the Father and God the Son.

From an ontological perspective, it is instructive that the post-baptismal revelation of the Trinity in Matt 3:16–17 occurs instantaneously and that the simultaneous actions are personally distinct between the three persons. God the Father speaks his approval to his beloved Son for receiving his commission, and God the Holy Spirit comes from the Father in the form of a dove upon God the Son. The simultaneous presence of the three divine persons indicates a dynamic and ongoing relationship between them. The Spirit is personal, just as the Father and the Son are personal, for there is communion between the Three. The glimpse we are granted of the trinitarian communion at his baptism is focused upon the Son, with the Spirit proceeding from the Father to the Son.

In Matt 10:20, Jesus exhorted the disciples to trust "the Spirit of your Father." The Holy Spirit comes from the Father, who is himself God. The intimate relation between the Father, the Son, and the Spirit thereby comprises the divine life into which Jesus's own disciples are invited to find peace. Notice similarly the pneumatic and trinitarian grounds undergirding Jesus's claim of authority in Matt 12:28. First, the Spirit is "of God" just as the kingdom is "of God." The Holy Spirit is the Executor of the Father's will, just as the kingdom is where the Father's will is executed. Second, Jesus is the Son of the living Father (16:16–17), who proclaims the kingdom and brings the kingdom to fallen humanity. Third, the Son and the Spirit are active on behalf of "God," who is in this passage understood to be the Father. Through such teaching, Matthew reminds us of the internal relations between the Spirit and the other two persons of the Trinity.

One of the most important conversations during which Jesus dealt with the deity of the Son and of the Spirit occurred after a series of controversies with the Jewish leaders of Jerusalem. This series began when Jesus entered Jerusalem. The crowds enthusiastically called out in front of his procession on a donkey and its foal, "Hosanna to the Son of David!" The chief priests and the scribes objected to Jesus allowing this, due to its clear messianic implications. However, Jesus cited Scripture to show his approval of the crowds (Matt 21:9, 15–16). Later, the Pharisees and Sadducees took turns trying to best Jesus in reference to the law (22:15–22, 23–33, 34–40). After they had been overwhelmed by him, the Lord asked them a final question from one of the psalms of David. He began with a question, "What do you think about the Messiah? Whose Son is he?" They, of course, pointed to David (v. 42).

Jesus then led them to consider the proper interpretation of Ps 110:1. "How is it then that David, inspired by the Spirit, calls him 'Lord'?" (v. 43). The point that Jesus was making is that David, as the king promised an eternal throne through the prophet Nathan, should be seen as superior to anyone, including his offspring (2 Sam 7:16). Yet David described his own son as *kyrios*, "Lord" (Matt 22:45). How could David assign to his descendant a superiority to himself? The Jewish leaders were unable to answer, for they did not understand that the Messiah is more than "the Son of David" (cf. Rom 1:3). Unless one perceives that the Messiah is also "the Son of God," the God whom Jesus identified for himself as "my Father in heaven" (Matt 16:16–17), one cannot perceive what Ps 110:1 means. Later, having obtained a mental if not spiritual perception, the high priest dramatically convicted Jesus of "blasphemy" for entitling himself "the Messiah, the Son of God," and "the Son of Man" (Matt 26:63–65; cf. Dan 7:13–14). According to Jesus, the Messiah is greater than the greatest person in Israel, David, because the Messiah is also the Son of God.

Jesus was put to death for what the Jews considered blasphemy, because this man made himself equal with God through his self-description as "the Son of God" (Matt 27:40, 43). Jesus taught that he and the Father shared in Godhead. And Jesus continued to teach, in three additional ways to those already described, that the Spirit shared in the Godhead. First, when referring to David's prophecy, he said David spoke *en pneumati*, "by the Spirit" (22:43). The eternal

Spirit whom Jesus knew was the same Spirit whom David knew. The inspiration of Scripture over the centuries demands a Spirit who transcends time itself. Second, it will be remembered that Jesus said blasphemy "against the Son of Man" could be forgiven, but not "blasphemy against the Holy Spirit" (12:31–32). Because a person could be confused at first by the humanity of the Son, a preliminary blasphemy against Christ as man might be forgiven. However, premeditated blasphemy against the deity himself could not be forgiven, and to blaspheme the Spirit is to blaspheme God.

The final way Jesus taught that the Holy Spirit shared fully in the deity of the Father and the Son was through the Great Commission. After his death and his resurrection from the dead, the Lord appeared to his disciples. Just as he had been commissioned by the Father to preach, so the Son commissioned his disciples to preach the coming of the kingdom of God in Christ. While doing so, the disciples were to make other disciples. They were then to immerse these new believers in "the name of God" (Matt 28:19) through baptism.

This initiatory religious act, baptism, signified a new definition of their identity according to this God. The "name" of God, being singular, identified this God as the one true God. The three personal names that were then attached to "the name" identified this God as also threefold. The Gospel according to Matthew ends with an important claim, an explicit affirmation made as part of the initial act of Christian worship, that one's baptism is in the name "of the Father and of the Son and of the Holy Spirit."[15] The Holy Spirit shares fully in the deity of the Father and of the Son. The co-deity of the Spirit

---

[15] For a fuller discussion of the trinitarian exegesis required in the Great Commission, see Yarnell, *God the Trinity*, ch. 1.

will be made even more explicit by the apostle John, to whose Gospel we turn in the next chapter.

Summary

The identity of the Spirit of God received clarity through the Gospel of Matthew. The Spirit of God is preeminently the Spirit of Jesus Christ. Matthew emphasized four ways the Spirit relates to Christ. First, the Spirit was the Conceiver of Christ. The Holy Spirit came over Mary in a holy manner and united the Son of God with humanity in her womb. Second, the Spirit was the Commissioner of Christ. The Spirit of God came upon Jesus at his baptism to anoint him for his ministry among God's people. Third, the Spirit is the Companion of Christ. The Holy Spirit accompanied Jesus Christ throughout his ministry, empowering him for his various activities of teaching with authority, defeating the demonic, and healing the people. Fourth, the Spirit shares in deity with Christ. The Holy Spirit and the Son are equally God in essence and in work. The Father's Spirit is the Son's Spirit.

The deity of the Holy Spirit and his intimate person-to-person relationship with the Son of God should shape our understanding of who God is and how God acts. We simply may not divide God the Trinity into pieces; at the same time, we simply may not confuse the persons of the Trinity. *The distinct persons of the Trinity may not be encountered by humanity apart from an encounter with the entire Godhead as one, for God is One yet Three.* The theological implications deriving from this fundamental truth are significant and multiple. For instance, from the perspective of personal conversion, it should be clear, therefore, that one does not receive Christ separately from receiving the Holy Spirit. In particular, baptism with the Holy Spirit should not be divided from saving faith in Jesus as

Lord. The human may not confess Christ Jesus as Lord apart from the work of the Holy Spirit (1 Cor 12:3). Likewise, as we have just discussed at length in this chapter, only Jesus may give a person the baptism of the Holy Spirit. As a result of this complex truth, it would be judicious for us not to divide the work of the Trinity, just as we should not divide the persons of the Trinity.

CHAPTER 5

Who Is This Person?
Insights from the Gospel of John

C lement of Alexandria famously referred to the Gospel of John as
a *pneumatikon euangelion*, a "spiritual gospel." Clement's use
of this phrase generated debate in the modern period over whether
John should be seen as less than reliable with regard to history.
However, Clement may have meant only that John wrote with more
theological intensity than the Synoptics, which, he granted, are more
historical in approach.[1] On the other hand, perhaps all Clement
intended to say was that John's Gospel was inspired, for his fuller
statement says that John, "divinely moved by the Spirit, composed
a spiritual Gospel."[2] A third option is that Clement might have been
observing that the Gospel of John has plenty to say about the Holy
Spirit in relation. Whatever Clement's cryptic intent, we can agree,

---

[1] Donald A. Carson, *The Gospel according to John*, The Pillar New Testament
Commentary (Grand Rapids, MI: Eerdmans, 1991), 28-29. Cf. Andreas J. Kösten-
berger, *A Theology of John's Gospel and Letters* (Grand Rapids, MI: Zondervan,
2009), 39.

[2] From Clement of Alexandria, *Hypotyposeis*; cited in Eusebius, *Ecclesiastical
History*, 6.14.7

either in the sense of theology or inspiration or pneumatology, that the Gospel of John is a "spiritual gospel."

What did John teach about the Holy Spirit? And how did he convey that teaching? John the Evangelist used a relational method to teach us about the identity of the Spirit. We can tell much about a person through the origin, form, and goal of their relationships. For instance, when a job applicant tells you where he was previously employed, as well as his title and length of employment, you get a decent measure of who he is almost immediately. Discovering where he has been living for the last five years also indicates something important about him. But when you glimpse a person's family relationships, that tells you a great deal more. In similar ways, we can learn much about who the Holy Spirit is through examining his relationships, including their origin, their intimacy, their purpose, and their tenor.

Theologians and philosophers have steadily recovered the ancient truth that a "person" is a being who finds his or her identity in relation to other persons.[3] The early church fathers utilized the language of *hupostasis* (Greek) and *personam* (Latin), "person," to arrive at a better understanding of who God is, who Christ is, and who human beings are. Personhood is where the orthodox definition of God as Trinity is settled. As many pastors today rightly teach, "God is three persons and one Being." Personhood is also where the orthodox definition of Jesus Christ as fully God and fully human finds its coherence, for Christ is "one person with two natures." The

---

[3] Carlyle Marney, *The Recovery of the Person*, 2nd ed. (Nashville: Abingdon, 1979); John D. Zizioulas, *Being as Communion: Studies in Personhood and the Church* (Crestwood, NY: St. Vladimir's Seminary Press, 1997); Robert Spaemann, *Persons: The Difference between "Someone" and "Something,"* trans. Oliver J. O'Donovan (New York: Oxford University Press, 2006); Roger Scruton, *The Face of God: The Gifford Lectures 2010* (New York: Continuum, 2012).

two natures of Jesus consist of his deity and his humanity, which find their unity in his one person. Christianity, in its confessional roots, therefore, deems the concept of personhood to be central to the definition of theological orthodoxy.

When we turn from the doctrines of the Trinity and of Christ to the doctrine of the Holy Spirit, we find the language of personhood is again very useful. The Spirit is both "personal," in that he is capable of relating to other persons, and a "person," in that his identity is substantiated by his relations to other persons. The Gospel of John, especially the Paraclete passages of chapters 14–16, reveals a great deal about the various relationships of the Holy Spirit. As we review the spiritual gospel, please note especially the prepositions, verbs, and nouns that indicate the Spirit's relationships. Ask yourself what they say about the identity of the Holy Spirit as a person. What are his titles? What does he do? How does he relate to others? Who is this person? By listening to God through the text, you will find that the Holy Spirit relates in different ways to God, to the church, and to the world. These relations help us understand who the Holy Spirit is as a person.

We shall now explore the insights that the Gospel of John conveys regarding the personhood of the Holy Spirit, specifically:

- the Spirit in relation to God,
- the Spirit in relation to believers, and
- the Spirit in relation to the world.

The Spirit in Relation to God

From a trinitarian and literary perspective, the first half of John's Gospel (chapters 1–13) is concerned primarily with the relationship of the Father and the Son. It is with the second half of the Gospel (especially chapters 14–16) that the Spirit's relational identity comes to the fore in a major way. However, there still are numerous significant references to the Holy Spirit in the earlier part. There are six episodes, as we shall see, in the first half of the John's Gospel that deal with the Holy Spirit, and each builds on the previous ones to demonstrate the relation of the Spirit to God the Trinity.

Pneumatic Episodes in the First Part of the Gospel. The first time the Holy Spirit is mentioned is with the baptism of Jesus by John the Baptist. The witness of the Baptist is that the Father gave him a special revelation regarding the significance of Jesus. Moreover, like Jesus himself in the Synoptics, John the Baptist also saw the Spirit descend and rest upon Jesus (John 1:32). The coming of Holy Spirit, as in the Synoptics, was in the form of a dove, likewise reflecting the imagery of a hovering bird already detailed in our interpretation of Gen 1:2. The remaining of the Spirit upon Jesus is also important to the Baptist. "He who sent me to baptize with water told me, 'The one you see the Spirit descending and resting on—he is the one who baptizes with the Holy Spirit'" (John 1:33). The visible coming of the Spirit upon Jesus was intended to give John the Baptist "certainty" that this was the one he had been told to expect.[4] As with the Synoptic witness, therefore, the baptism of Jesus involves an explicitly trinitarian account—the Father, the Son, and the Holy Spirit are equally and contemporaneously evident.

The Trinitarian placement of the work of the Holy Spirit continues in the other episodes referring to the Spirit in the teaching of Jesus or of the evangelist during the first half of the Gospel of John. In the second episode, Jesus, the second person of the Trinity, tells Nicodemus that the kingdom of God, defined here as the personal

---

[4] F.F. Bruce, *The Gospel of John: Introduction, Exposition, and Notes* (Grand Rapids: Eerdmans, 1983), 54.

rule of the first person of the Trinity, cannot be experienced by humanity apart from being "born over again" or "born from above" (John 3:3, 7).[5] To be born in this way is a work that only the Holy Spirit could do, for the Lord Jesus refers to it also as being "born of the Spirit" (vv. 5, 6, 8). Theologians refer to being "born again" as "regeneration," and we see from Jesus's words that regeneration clearly is the sovereign act of the Holy Spirit.

In the third pneumatic episode, after another discourse from John the Baptist regarding the primacy of the Son (vv. 27–30), John the evangelist reaffirms the primacy of the Son in relation to the coming of the Spirit. The Father sent the Son to speak the Father's words, and the Son in turn gives the Spirit in simultaneity with the words. "For the one whom God sent speaks God's words, since he gives the Spirit without measure" (v. 34). This passage tells us three things about the shape of the trinitarian work in the ministry of Jesus: First, Jesus Christ is the Son whom God the Father sends. Second, Jesus is the One who speaks God's words. Third, the Son is the One who gives the Holy Spirit without any diminution. The Father sent the Son fully into this world, and the Son sends the Spirit alongside the words of the Father to inundate the lives of believers.

In the fourth episode, the second person of the Trinity indicates that the first person of the Trinity may be worshiped only through the third person of the Trinity: "The true worshipers will worship the Father in Spirit and in truth" (4:23). After noting the substantial nature of God as spiritual, Jesus again employed *en*[6] to restate the necessity of worshiping through the person of the Spirit (v. 24).

---

[5] The Greek *anothen* could convey either or both "born over again" or "born from above."

[6] *En* can be translated into English as "in." This preposition can be understood in the sense of a location (as in, "I am in the room") or in the sense of an instrument (as in, "I am worshiping in the Spirit.")

Commentators have disagreed over whether the various occurrences of the divine *pneuma* in this episode are best taken in a personal, substantial, or even functional way.[7] For instance, Baptist scholar George R. Beasley-Murray sees the references here as both personal and functional rather than substantial.[8] But Donald A. Carson, a Reformed evangelical theologian, incorporates the personal and substantial senses.[9] Due to the unsupportable anti-metaphysical bias infecting the Anglo–German tradition of biblical theology, I concur with Carson rather than Beasley-Murray at this point.[10] However, significantly, both Carson and Beasley-Murray agree that the personal nature of the Spirit of God must be affirmed: human beings engage in the true worship of God only in and through the person of the Holy Spirit.

In the fifth episode that reveals the identity and function of the Holy Spirit, we see the defining work of the Spirit is intimately associated with both Christology and anthropology (the doctrines of the Messiah and of humanity). These associations arise with the definition of the primary work of the Spirit, but they also tell us something about the person of the Spirit vis-à-vis the Father and the Son. John

---

[7] The personal understanding focuses on *pneuma* as a living person. The functional understanding focuses on *pneuma* as an activity. The substantial understanding focuses on *pneuma* as spiritual versus material.

[8] "'God is Spirit,' defines God, not in his metaphysical being, but 'according to his work in the world.'" George R. Beasley-Murray, *John*, Word Biblical Commentary (Waco, TX: Word Books, 1987), 62.

[9] On the one hand, *pneuma* is taken substantially in this passage to mean "that God is invisible, divine as opposed to human, life-giving and unknowable to human beings unless he chooses to reveal himself." On the other hand, *pneuma* refers to the Holy Spirit, for worship is "made possible by the gift of the Holy Spirit." Carson, *The Gospel according to John*, 225.

[10] For a summative critique of the modern historical critical method that has handicapped much of evangelical exegesis, see Yarnell, *God the Trinity*, 88–96 (see chap. 4, n. 3).

6:63 states, "The Spirit is the one who gives life. The flesh doesn't help at all. The words that I have spoken to you are spirit and are life." The Father, it will be remembered, gave the words to Jesus (3:34). So new life comes to the redeemed from God through the words of Jesus and through the presence of the Spirit, for the Spirit "gives life" even as the words themselves are "spirit and life." The close relationship of the Spirit and the words, which come from the Father through the Son, teach an intimacy of agency between the persons that points toward an intimacy of personhood. The words come from the Father to the Son, and the Spirit accompanies the words of the Son. The Father, the Son, and the Holy Spirit are united in their shared divine work of revelation and in their shared divine identity. Humans cannot understand revelation without reference to all three persons of the Godhead.

During the sixth episode, the relations of the Father with the Son and the Spirit recede into the background in order for the relation between the Son and the Spirit to receive attention. Typically, the apostle dwelled on the working of the Spirit, but "economy" naturally reflects a preexisting "ontology." The term "economy of the Spirit" captures how the Spirit acts or works, but the activity or work of a person presupposes the preexisting reality of that person. The term "ontology" considers that underlying reality, the being of a person, in this case the person of the Spirit. In the sixth pneumatic episode from the first half of the spiritual gospel, we must perceive who the Spirit is through what he does. Jesus said that the "one who believes in me" will have "streams of living water flow from deep within him" (7:38). The evangelist added, in an interpretive note, "He said this about the Spirit. Those who believed in Jesus were going to receive the Spirit" (v. 39). Personal faith in Jesus Christ, the Son of God, arises from the personal interior presence of the Holy Spirit of God within the human being. The Spirit is the one who personally and sovereignly places the source of life, who is God, into the very soul of the human being. The interwoven relations indicated by the way God brings new new life to the human are profound and complex and demand careful consideration.

Trinitarian Chronology. In an important programmatic note at the conclusion of the sixth pneumatic episode, the evangelist then added, "for the Spirit had not yet been given because Jesus had not yet been glorified" (v. 39). The ontology of the Spirit in his relationship to the Son, therefore, seemed to be a matter of some importance to the evangelist. While there is an undeniably close intimacy between the Spirit and the Son, there is also a differentiation that must be maintained. The reference to Jesus being "glorified" concerns his crucifixion and resurrection, critical events that he absolutely must undergo before returning to the Father's glory (cf. 13:31–32). Moreover, God the Spirit will not come until after God the Son has returned to God the Father. How does this work in time?

The Spirit of God, who will bring the kingdom of God into human hearts, must wait to do his work until after the Son of God has completed his great work of death, resurrection, and ascension. As Beasley-Murray pithily summarized this unsurpassable doctrine, "The crucial event whereby the saving sovereignty came among men was the crucifixion–resurrection of Jesus."[11] The Holy Spirit comes upon Jesus and remains. Jesus gives the Holy Spirit in fullness through baptizing his followers in the Spirit, bringing them to new life through the new birth. The Holy Spirit will remain with the disciples of Christ, but he may not come in a regenerative fashion until after Christ has performed his works of cross, resurrection, and ascension. There is no regeneration, which is another way to speak

---

[11] Beasley-Murray, *John*, 117.

of baptism with the Holy Spirit, apart from the saving work of the incarnate Son of God.

In the second half of the Gospel, Jesus reinforced the necessity of his departure in order for the Spirit to come among men: "It is for your benefit that I go away, because if I don't go away the Counselor will not come to you" (16:7). Finally, after his death and resurrection, and immediately before his ascension, only then did the Son actually, if proleptically, give to his disciples the gift of the Spirit (20:22). A conflation or confusion between the Son and the Spirit must be avoided. The Holy Spirit does not come upon the church until after the Son has returned to the Father. The coming of the Spirit at Pentecost must defer to the death, resurrection, and ascension of the Son.

The Paraclete Sayings. The densest concentration of references to the Holy Spirit in the second half of John occurs in chapters 14–16. The personal and economic relations of the Holy Spirit receive further definition through these so-called Paraclete sayings, which are contained in these pivotal chapters known among scholars as "the Farewell Discourse." We can count five distinct sayings about the Paraclete, though the last two are adjacent to one another. The Greek word that Jesus used to teach about the Spirit's identity is *Parakletos*, which might be translated as "Helper," "Comforter," or "Advocate." But it is probably best rendered as "Counselor," following the Revised Standard Version and the Christian Standard Bible. The latter translation allows both the interpersonal and legal dimensions of this relational term to come to the fore.[12]

The trinitarian dimensions of the term *Parakletos* can be found in that the Spirit is referred to as "another Counselor" (14:16). While

---

[12] For the subtleties in translation of *parakletos*, consult Moisés Silva, *New International Dictionary of New Testament Theology and Exegesis*, 2nd ed. (Grand Rapids: Zondervan, 2014), 3:627–33.

debated, it has been argued that Jesus used the adjective *allon* here, rather than *heteron*, to modify *parakleton* in order to teach that the Spirit is "another of the same type" as opposed to being "another of a different kind."[13] Complicating our understanding, yet illuminating our theology, is the fact that the term *parakletos* is not reserved exclusively for the Spirit in the canon. Jesus is referred to in the first letter of John as a *Parakleton* (1 John 2:1). And while the noun *parakletos* is never used of God the Father, the Father does engage in the activity of *paraklesis*, or "comfort." Paul praised God the Father as the origin or fount of all comfort. "Blessed be the God and Father of our Lord Jesus Christ, the Father of mercies and the God of all comfort" (2 Cor 1:3). All three persons—the Father, the Son, and the Spirit—apparently engage together in the ministry of *paraklesis*, "comfort," even as the Spirit and the Son are entitled *Parakletoi*, "Comforters" or "Counselors."

Within the New Testament, the most detailed aspects of the Holy Spirit's eternal relations to God the Father and the Son are provided within these Paraclete sayings. (We will consider the Spirit's relation to believers and unbelievers in the following two sections.) In the first saying, the divine perfection of eternality is ascribed to the Spirit through the promise that the Spirit who gives life will reside with the disciples "forever" (*eis ton aiona*, "into perpetuity"; John 14:16). In the second saying, Jesus begins, "But the Counselor, the Holy Spirit, whom the Father will send in my name . . ." (v. 26). Here, the Father is acknowledged as the origin of the economic procession of the Spirit. The Son is the One whose "name," or personal identity, is cited as the reason for this economic procession.

In the third saying, Jesus provides both an economic description and an ontological description of the origin of the Spirit in the

---

[13] Carson, *The Gospel according to John*, 499–500.

world. "When the Counselor comes, the one I will send to you from the Father—the Spirit of truth who proceeds from the Father—he will testify of me" (15:26). The Spirit comes into the world to do his work because the Son said, "*Pempso*," or, "I will send," him into the world. Economically, therefore, the Son is involved in the origination of the Spirit, for the Spirit comes and works due to the initiative of the Son. The Father shares in this economic sending, too, for the Spirit also comes into the world "from the Father" (*para tou patros*).

However, behind and beyond the economic and functional perspective is the ontological and eternal reality. Eternally, Jesus stated, the Spirit specifically originates with the Father. The Spirit "proceeds" (*ekporeuetai*) "from the Father" (*para tou patros*). The Nicene Creed properly assigns great weight to the terminology of this text, for John 15:26, the third Paraclete saying, is the only biblical text that explicitly labels the eternal relation of the Spirit to God. God the Spirit's "procession" manifestly originates "with" or "from" (*para*) God the Father.

The processional aspect of the Spirit's eternal relation has not occasioned significant controversy among orthodox Christians, but the origin of that relation certainly has. The theological division between Eastern Christianity and Western Christianity is at its most dogmatic with regard to the origin of the eternal procession of the Spirit. Following Augustine, the West adopted over time the position that the Spirit proceeds from both the Father and the Son (*filioque*, "and the Son," is the Latin addition to the Nicene Creed). But the East officially retained the original version of the creed, which states that the Spirit proceeds from the Father. For Western theologians, the Son is distinguished eternally by proceeding singly, from the Father, while the Spirit proceeds dually, from the Father and the Son. For Eastern theologians, the Son is distinguished from the Spirit by being eternally "generate" from the Father, while the Spirit eternally "proceeds" from the Father. The problem in reconciling the great traditions remains unsolved.

The fourth of the sayings about the Paraclete, like the third, affirms that the Son also "sends" the Spirit (16:7). Again, this concerns the economic procession rather than the eternal procession of the Spirit. However, Augustinians will often appeal to what has become known as "Rahner's axiom" to validate tightly equating the economic procession with the eternal procession. For Augustinians in the West, the procession of the Spirit from the Son depends on correlating the economic "sending" of the Spirit with the eternal "procession" of the Spirit. Equating the economic with the eternal remains the only theological basis for ascribing the procession of the Spirit to the Son.

In other words, a clear exegetical basis does not exist for the double procession of the Spirit. This remains true in spite of Augustine's appeals to the economic description of the Spirit shedding abroad God's love in our hearts in Rom 5:5 and to the ontological description of God as love in 1 John 4:8, 16.[14] In neither of these two instances is the Spirit directly identified as the eternal love between the Father and the Son. Describing the Spirit as personal love between the other two persons may provide positive pastoral benefits, and it may contribute dubious polemical points in ecclesiastical politics. However, in addition to the problem of a thin exegetical foundation, defining the Spirit as divine love may, but need not necessarily, risk making the Spirit the ontological base of the Godhead, thereby obfuscating the Spirit's distinct personhood.

The fifth of the Paraclete sayings provides a solid footing for the doctrine of one deity being shared equally and entirely by the three

---

[14] For more discussion regarding Augustine's theological exegesis of these passages, see Yarnell, "The Person and Work of the Holy Spirit," 506–7 (see intro., n. 1).

persons of the Trinity. The Father and the Son share whatever can be identified as "Mine"—whatever belongs to the Father also belongs to the Son. All that the Father possesses is also possessed by the Son. And the Holy Spirit, Jesus repeated for effect, has sovereign authority over everything that the Father and the Son personally possess. I have worked through the exegetical aspects and discussed the trinitarian significance of this passage in my book *God the Trinity* and refer you to that work for more detail.[15]

Taken together and in summary, the five sayings of Jesus regarding the Spirit as *Parakleton* suggest four theological rules for identifying the deity of the Spirit:

1. The Holy Spirit proceeds eternally from the Father. By reason of theological extension, it could perhaps be argued that the Spirit proceeds from the Son too. I personally prefer to speak of the Spirit's eternal procession "from" the Father and "through" the Son, granting Rahner's axiom a secondary validity.

2. The Holy Spirit is sent economically by both the Son and the Father, the latter of whom sends the Spirit at the Son's request.

3. The Holy Spirit shares equally in the divine perfections of comfort, eternality, and sovereignty with the Father and the Son. The Spirit may thus be said to be fully divine with the other two persons of the Trinity.

4. The Spirit and the Son must be perceived as intimately related in both being and work, but the two persons must be maintained simultaneously as different. This truth of eternal distinction extends theologically to the Father as well.

---

[15] Yarnell, *God the Trinity*, 107–33.

The Spirit in Relation to Believers

When we turn to the relationship of the Spirit to believers in Jesus Christ, we first notice that while the Father and the Son relate to the Spirit in an ontological unity, the unity of God with believers is radically different. Of course, believers are united with the Spirit in a highly intimate way. This is the import of the promises that believers will:

- be baptized "with the Holy Spirit" (John 1:33),
- receive the Spirit "without measure" (3:34),
- worship "in Spirit" (4:23), and
- have the Spirit "flow from deep within" (7:38).

These early promises are reinforced in the Paraclete sayings with further promises that the Counselor will "come to you" (16:7) and that he "remains with you and will be in you" (14:17). Finally, the blessing of the disciples with the continuing presence of the Spirit begins with the personal action of the divine breath emanating from the human mouth of the Son of God (20:22). However, the promises themselves, reinforced by the delay in the disciples' reception of the Spirit, indicate that believers' unity with the Holy Spirit comes by gift and not by right. The oneness of the Spirit with believers results from a work of grace and not because of a shared nature. In this way, the Holy Spirit's immanence with believers does not compromise his transcendence over them.

The union of the Holy Spirit with believers begins eternally in the sovereign will of God and temporally with regeneration. Human beings do not control the Holy Spirit in the process of being born again. Jesus drew upon the physical meanings of the Greek verb *pneo*, "breathe" or "blow," and its related noun *pneuma*, "breath" or "wind." His use of these terms carries similar connotations to their appearance in the Hebrew Old Testament. Jesus employs them as "vigorous metaphors" in order to emphasize sovereignty.[16] "The wind blows where it pleases, and you hear its sound, but you don't know where it comes from or where it is going. So it is with everyone who is born of the Spirit" (3:8). Regeneration is a work of grace enacted without reference to human working. This does not mean that regeneration occurs apart from faith and repentance, for human faith and human repentance are also requisite. A contextual literary reading of John 3:1–13 (on the necessity of regeneration) alongside verses 14–18 (on the necessity of faith) and verses 19–21 (on the necessity of repentance) will demonstrate their concomitance in the human subject.

Not only does the Spirit begin the life of new believers; he continues as an empowering presence in their lives. As previously indicated, the Holy Spirit accompanies the words of Jesus as an effective agent in the believing subject. He creates new life through those words. Jesus continually buttresses his claim that the life-giving work of the Spirit is not due in any way to human nature: "The flesh doesn't help at all" (6:63). Again, the Spirit enables believers to engage in true worship (4:23–24). And again, the Spirit will come to live within believers, working like "a well of water springing up in him for eternal life" (4:14; cf. 7:38). The early references in the Gospel of John thus teach that the beginning and the continuance of the Christian life remain the personal work of the Holy Spirit.

The Paraclete sayings also accentuate the Spirit's work of revelation to believers. The Counselor is "the Spirit of truth" (14:17; 15:26; 16:13; cf. Jesus Christ as "truth," 14:6). The role of the Spirit

---

[16] Silva, *New International Dictionary of New Testament Theology and Exegesis*, 3:820–21.

of truth is primarily among the apostles, but secondarily among believers after them. He will "teach you all things and remind you of everything I have told you" (14:26), Jesus said. Jesus told his disciples that they were, at that time, incapable of receiving all that he could tell them. But, he promised, "when the Spirit of truth comes, he will guide you into all the truth" (16:13). The Spirit of truth would speak whatever he heard from the Father and the Son. He would declare both the past and the future to the disciples. And his intention in such teaching would be to "glorify" the Son (v. 14). The revelatory work of the Spirit in the apostles' teaching continues today through the texts they wrote, texts that the church collected into the New Testament. While the ultimate end of the Spirit's revelatory ministry is the believers' glorification of the Son of God, the penultimate goal is their testimony to the world (15:26). To the Spirit's testimony to the world we now turn.

The Spirit in Relation to the World

While the first half of the Gospel of John focused primarily on the regeneration of believers, the latter half turns increasingly to a concern with the world from which the unbelievers are drawn into faith. The Spirit of God in the Paraclete sayings is the Counselor who assists the disciples. He is also the "Spirit of truth" who utilizes the disciples to bring truth to the world. The world, in its natural and fallen state, is "unable to receive him because it doesn't see him or know him." The disciples, however, may testify to the world about God, because the disciples of Jesus know the Spirit even as the world does not know the Spirit (14:17). Through such testimony, the Spirit encounters the world, in spite of its total ignorance of him. The Spirit draws close to the world and uses the disciples to "testify" to the world about Jesus. Jesus said that the Counselor, who will come upon the disciples during the baptism of the church at Pentecost, "will testify about me. You also will testify, because you have been with me from the beginning" (15:26c–27).

The promise that the Spirit would guide the apostles to remember the teachings of Jesus is significant for the life of the church since their days. Not only were they promised the ability to remember Christ's teachings, which are centered upon his death and resurrection. They were also promised that they would be led by the Spirit to know the future work of God. The dialectic between the historical teachings of Jesus to the church and the theological proclamations of the church to the world requires the superintending presence of the Holy Spirit. The Spirit inspired the apostles to write the New Testament books, and their writings still serve us today. The apostles, who were with Jesus, who heard Jesus, who then remembered him perfectly, and who knew the meaning of Christ's doctrine for the future, were accompanied and empowered in their witness by the Holy Spirit.

The apostles Peter and Paul later provided more detail regarding the inspiration and the authority of the New Testament writings by the Holy Spirit (2 Tim 3:15–17; 2 Pet 1:19–21). But it is the apostle John who provides a dynamic pneumatic and evangelistic account of the means and ends of Scripture's inspiration. If the Spirit had not led the apostles to remember the words of Christ and to record them in written form, we would not have the authoritative text we now possess. This text, the Holy Bible, is the intended means for continuing to spread the world-changing apostolic testimony to Christ. Scripture is the contemporary means of the Spirit's testimony through the prophets and apostles.

But what exactly does the Spirit do with the testimony of the apostles before the world? In the fourth saying, we are provided with a dynamic description of the Spirit's work in relation to the world. "When he comes, he will convict the world about sin, righteousness, and judgment" (John 16:8). The Spirit's ministry to the world is one of "exposing."[17] While the world wrongly tried Jesus, the Holy Spirit puts the world itself on trial before God. The Spirit's legal ministry as *Parakletos* turns from one of comforting and advocating on behalf of believers toward a legal ministry of exposing or convicting the sins of the world to divine judgment.

The Counselor's work of conviction is described in three acts: sin, righteousness, and judgment. First, the world's "sin" is definitively that it does not believe in Christ. Unbelief in the good news of Jesus is what removes the world from divine grace. Unbelief is the primary sin. Second, the world is told that "righteousness" rose from the dead and ascended to the right hand of the Father. The righteous Judge himself is the one previously convicted by the world. The world's only hope resides in turning to the Judge and receiving his personal righteousness by faith. The prominent role of Jesus as Judge in such passages as this may encourage some systematic theologians to consider including judgment within his role of Kingship. Another option might include recognizing a fourth office alongside that of prophet, priest, and king, mirroring the time of the Judges before the Israelite monarchy. In whatever way formulated, the Holy Spirit clearly works with the Son in revealing and enforcing divine judgment.

According to Jesus, the third work of the Spirit with regard to "judgment" is to convict people that "the ruler of this world has been judged." This world's ruler, the serpent who led humanity into sin (Genesis 3), has been weighed, found wanting, and eternally condemned through the victory of Christ on the cross. The only hope

---

[17] George R. Beasley-Murray, *The Gospel of Life: Theology in the Fourth Gospel* (Peabody, MA: Hendrickson, 1991), 76–77.

for those in the world is a shift of allegiance from this world to the kingdom of God. If those who reside in the world wish to receive salvation—to be transferred from one kingdom to another—they must come to know and submit to Jesus Christ. Testifying to such God-given knowledge about Jesus Christ is the work of the church empowered by the Holy Spirit.

Summary

In the Gospel of John, the personal identity of the Holy Spirit is revealed through his relationships with other persons. The Holy Spirit is the sovereign, transcendent, and eternal God; at the same time he is also the comforting, immanent, and revealing God. The Spirit proceeds eternally from, at least, God the Father, and he is sent into the world by God the Father and God the Son. The Son needed to return to the Father before the Spirit could come to the disciples. He is thereafter sent into the world to bring faith, repentance, and regeneration to the followers of the Son through indwelling them personally. The Holy Spirit also has a ministry of revelation through the apostles, a ministry captured literarily in the perfect text of the New Testament. Finally, John teaches us that the Holy Spirit carries on a ministry of testimony through exposing to the world the truth about the existence and gravity of human sin, about the righteousness available in Jesus Christ, and about God's judgment of evil.

If God the Holy Spirit is personal in his identity, as the Gospel of John so clearly teaches, then what does this mean to you personally? *The personal nature of God the Holy Spirit means that he is concerned with you, not merely from the frightening perspective of his transcendent otherness, but from the comforting perspective of his intimate nearness.* The Father, the Son, and the Holy Spirit eternally face one another in their loving unity and graceful threeness.

Out of such inherent love for the persons of one another, God chose to create other persons in his triune image (Gen 1:26–28). Human beings were created in the triune God's image so as to rule creation for him, but we chose to rebel with Satan and rule for ourselves (Gen 3:6). Our rebellion against the divine persons sundered our relation with God.

However, God's sovereign love was not to be conquered. The divine person of the Father sent the divine person of the Son to unite with our humanity permanently in the incarnation (John 3:17). The Son then died for our sins and arose from death for our justification (Rom 4:25), offering us life through faith in him (John 20:30). Subsequently, to bring human beings personally into eternal relationship with God, the Father and the Son sent the divine person of the Holy Spirit to convict us of our sin, of the coming judgment, and of the righteousness available through faith in Jesus Christ (John 16:7–11). The Spirit now comes to dwell within us through inundating us in himself by regeneration (John 3:6), uniting us with the Son by faith (John 15:26; 16:13–14). He enables us to return to the loving presence of the Father in the blessed vision of light for which we were originally created (John 1:5–8; 8:12; 12:35–36; Rev 22:5).[18] From the apostle John's enlightening doctrine of the person of the Holy Spirit to the apostle Paul's beautiful description of the identity of the Spirit we now turn.

---

[18] Hans Boersma, *Seeing God: The Beatific Vision in Christian Tradition* (Grand Rapids: Eerdmans, 2018).

CHAPTER 6

Who Is the Holy Spirit to Believers? Insights from Romans 8

"Among the New Testament writers, Paul deserves the title 'theologian of the Spirit,' for he gives the most comprehensive and integrated teaching on this topic."[1] While one could perhaps ascribe that title to the apostle John instead of the apostle Paul, biblical scholar and translator Moisés Silva makes a valid point. That the ascription of that title is applied to the most prolific New Testament writer also highlights the complexity in treating Paul summarily. It would be difficult to write a comprehensive chapter on the doctrine of the Holy Spirit according to the apostle Paul due to the immense amount of material one would be required to cover. Complicating the matter yet further is that Paul treats the Spirit not only in a "comprehensive" way but also in an "integrated" way, as Silva stated.

Comprehending Paul's Pneumatology. If Paul had jotted down a pneumatic system, we might have found an easy way forward, but Paul never penned a systematic theology. Rather, like every great pastor, he set out to address the critical needs of the church for

---

[1] Silva, *New International Dictionary of New Testament Theology and Exegesis*, 3:815 (see chap. 5, n. 12).

which God had made him responsible. Paul's writings, therefore, do not lend themselves easily to a comprehensive theological exegesis of his doctrine of the Spirit, though some have tried to develop such from them. On the more extensive side, Gordon Fee wrote a 991-page exposition of the Holy Spirit in the letters of Paul.[2] In a more summative mode, I once outlined Paul's treatment of the Spirit according to the loci of systematic theology: "revelation, the Trinity, anthropology and hamartiology, Christ, soteriology, the Christian life and the church, and eschatology."[3] Eschewing either the comprehensive exegetical strategy or the summative systematic strategy, other scholars have limited themselves to tracing a specific way that Paul treats the Spirit in relation to the life of the churches. Such a strategy proves helpful, for Paul was primarily interested in the Spirit with regard to the Christian life. For instance, some have chronologically followed Paul's progress in his use of the Greek word *pneumatikos*.

Pneumatikos designates something "spiritual" or "in relation to the Spirit." At first, in the Thessalonian correspondence, Paul discussed the Spirit in relation to the end time. But, significantly, he did not bring the Spirit into direct relationship with Christ. Afterwards, in the Corinthian correspondence, Paul reacted against the elitist claims of those who considered themselves *pneumatikoi*, "spiritual people," because they had been gifted with *pneumatikoi*, "spiritual things," or *charismata*, "spiritual gifts," especially the lesser gift of speaking in tongues. At this point, Paul felt compelled to reorient

---

[2] Gordon D. Fee, *God's Empowering Presence: The Holy Spirit in the Letters of Paul* (Peabody, MA: Hendrickson, 1994).

[3] Yarnell, "The Person and Work of the Holy Spirit," 495–98 (see intro., n. 1).

what it meant to be "spiritual" through a "christological (re)defini-tion of the Spirit."[4]

First, the apostle undermined the pretension of Christian elitism through claiming, like his opponents, "I think I also have the Holy Spirit" (1 Cor 7:40, paraphrased). Next, at the beginning of the Co-rinthian gifts discourse, Paul asserted that the necessarily universal Christian possession of the Spirit is what enables the saving confes-sion of Jesus as Lord (12:3). At the end of the same gifts discourse, he said those who are truly "spiritual" will agree that his writing, which prioritizes prophecy and delimits tongues for the common good,[5] "is the Lord's command" (14:37). Finally, in the resurrection discourse, Paul located the life-granting work of the Spirit exclu-sively within "the last Adam," Jesus Christ (15:45).

The elitist challenge to the unity of the church, and to ortho-dox Christocentrism in the Corinthian church, forced Paul to pay more attention to the Holy Spirit in people's lives. Over against the false spiritualist clique, the true *pneumatikos*, "spiritual person," is the Christian. And the Christian, who exists through faith alone in Christ alone, is the *pneumatikon*. Being spiritual is no more and no less than being in Christ. For Paul, there can be no special spiritual category that elevates some Christians above others. The remaining

---

[4] Alexander J. M. Wedderburn, "Pauline Pneumatology and Pauline Theology," in *The Holy Spirit and Christian Origins: Essays in Honor of James D. G. Dunn*, ed. Graham N. Stanton, Bruce W. Longenecker, and Stephen C. Barton (Grand Rapids: Eerdmans, 2004), 147.

[5] "Christology should control the Corinthians' assessment and use of their posses-sion of the Spirit. That Spirit was given for and to all of the Corinthian community, and the exercise of spiritual gifts should serve the good of all and the upbuilding of the whole community." Wedderburn, 151. For a similar approach to the problem of elitist spirituality in Paul's letters, see Silva, *New International Dictionary of New Testament Theology and Exegesis*, 3:818–20.

Pauline correspondence, including the letter to the Galatians, correlates with this general development.

While the progressive definition of *pneumatikos* in the Pauline corpus helpfully provides a thematic overview of the integration of the Spirit into the Christian life, it does not speak adequately to other important themes regarding the Spirit. One could, for instance, trace Paul's understanding of the term *pneuma* when it is used of human nature, when it is used with regard to the law, or when it is applied to the resurrection. However, due to the space available in this book, we have chosen to focus on one very significant Pauline text.

Integrating Identity with Activity. Romans 8 is the best candidate for a focused exegetical treatment due to its density of references to the Holy Spirit and due to its soteriological subject matter. *Pneuma* is used twenty-one times in this chapter, with nineteen of those instances indicating the divine Spirit. Most of the references to *pneuma* occur in the first half of the chapter, so that is where we will keep our attention. In addition, Paul's primary goal in this chapter is to describe the progress and end of salvation in Jesus Christ. Chapter 8 brings to a culmination Paul's profound delineation of "the main theme" of the canonically first, manifestly longest, and doubtlessly greatest letter of his writing career. And the main theme, according to a former bishop of Oxford, is the justification of sinners through faith in the righteousness of God displayed in the gospel of Jesus Christ.[6]

One factor complicating our intention to discover the identity of the Spirit through this chapter is that "Paul's focus is not so much on the Spirit as such, but on what the Spirit *does*." However, in spite of the significant difference between identity and activity,

---

[6] K.E. Kirk, *The Epistle to the Romans in the Revised Version: With Introduction and Commentary* (New York: Oxford University Press, 1937), 33–37, 176–218.

"this is perhaps the best way to learn about the Spirit."[7] Why would a biblical chapter devoted to the activity of the Spirit be a proper way to learn about the identity of the Spirit? If you will refer back to my daughter's brilliant comments in the preface, she provides the answer: "It is easier to talk about what somebody does than what somebody is. But what somebody does tells you about who they are." We indeed can learn about the essence or ontology of the Spirit through the work or economy of the Spirit. ("Ontology" is a philosophical term used to indicate that we are talking about what someone or something really *is*. "Economy" is a theological term used to indicate that we are talking about what someone *does*.) Moreover, in his characteristic manner of only subtly demonstrating his deep learning, the apostle Paul nonchalantly dropped very helpful clues regarding the ontology of the Spirit into the text of his letters, including Romans 8.

Death, Rejection, Hopelessness. The background to the dogmatic part of Romans that reaches a height with chapter 8 is concerned with the existential human problems of suffering, death, and hopelessness. From the severely limited perspective of human beings, the natural picture of reality with which one is confronted is hopelessness. People who do not possess biblical revelation do not see—cannot see—how the death that ends every bodily creature and the sufferings that increasingly consume our aging bodies may be overcome. All that we can naturally do with all of our arts and sciences and all of our accumulated knowledge is to demonstrate the futility of our efforts. Suffering awaits us before death. And what is beyond death but silence? "Absolute futility," cried the Teacher, because the only thing he could see from his natural perspective

---

[7] Douglas J. Moo, *The Epistle to the Romans*, The New International Commentary on the New Testament (Grand Rapids: Eerdmans, 1996), 468.

was emptiness, vanity. "Everything is futile" (Eccl 1:2). The human being without God's special revelation is confronted with such hopelessness.[8]

The situation for the person who has received the divine revelation of God's law might be seen as better. But if he receives the law and still disobeys, his situation is actually worse. The history of Israel, the elect people of God, from the days of Abraham through Moses to David and the prophets, like the history of all nations, is one massive failure to live according to God's law (Rom 1:18–2:24). The laments of David are taken up by Paul: "There is no one righteous, not even one. There is no one who understands, there is no one who seeks God" (Rom 3:10–11; cf. Ps 14:1–3; 53:1–3; Eccl 7:20). The crisis, however, is not in the perfect law of God, but with the foolish human heart (Ps 14:1; 53:1). This is why Ezekiel declared the only way forward for humanity was for God himself to "give you a new heart and put a new spirit within you" (Ezek 36:26). The replacement of the old, recalcitrant heart with a new, responsive heart can only happen because God will do this for humanity. "I will place my Spirit within you and cause you to follow my statutes and carefully observe my ordinances" (v. 27; cf. Jer 31:31–33).

The anthropological problem, which can be defined as an evil and unresponsive human spirit, requires a theological solution, the personal presence of the divine Spirit. *God the Father has elected to bring salvation to his wayward creatures by sending his Son and by sending his Spirit.* The only hope to defeat the sin, suffering, and death of the human being is through the victory of the cross, worked by the perfect human being, the Son of God, who was sent to become a man. But the victory worked through the atonement of

---

[8] Matthew Levering, *Dying and the Virtues* (Grand Rapids: Eerdmans, 2018), 29–48.

Christ on the cross can only become the individual person's possession through God's gift of participation. And that participation in Christ, that union with Christ, can only be worked by the Spirit of God. The human spirit has neither the will nor the ability to embrace the gift of Christ. The unaided human spirit lies helpless and hopeless in its ignorance, suffering, and impending death. But God's plan is to send his Spirit to bring to the human life (Rom 8:1–13), adoption (vv. 14–25), and intercession (vv. 26–27).

Romans 8 teaches us that the Holy Spirit is:

- the Spirit of life,
- the Spirit of adoption, and
- the Spirit of intercession.

The Spirit of Life

As noted before, while Paul discourses about the Holy Spirit with unparalleled thickness in Romans 8, his primary concern is with the Christian life. So, while Paul indeed provides a description of "the Spirit of life" in the first thirteen verses, his focus is on the *nomos* of the Spirit of life rather than the identity of the Spirit of life. *Nomos* here does not refer to the Mosaic "law" or any other law, but to a "principle."[9] The principle of the Spirit in the life of the Christian is this: *The Spirit is the one who creates life within the Christian through uniting us with Christ, who himself made life available for*

---

[9] Cranfield also dismisses the translation of *nomos* as "law" of the Spirit, preferring instead "the authority and constraint exercised upon believers by the Holy Spirit." C. E. B. Cranfield, *A Critical and Exegetical Commentary on the Epistle to the Romans*, International Critical Commentary, 2 vols. (New York: T&T Clark, 1975), 1:376. For the simpler translation of "principle of the Spirit and life" in contradistinction to "principle of sin and death," see Moo, *The Epistle to the Romans*, 473–77.

the Christian through his cross and his resurrection. Just as Christ worked our justification before God on the basis of what only he could do for us, the Holy Spirit works our union with God on the basis of what only he can do in us. The Holy Spirit's work in us is a work of creating life, of continuing that life, and of completing that life.

The creation of life within us, as well as its continuation and completion, is a divine act. Paul believed that only the Spirit of God could personally create the new life. All three persons of the one Godhead exercise agency in the granting of life to the believer from beginning to end. First, God the Father, "he who raised Christ from the dead," is the One who "will also bring your mortal bodies to life through his Spirit who lives in you" (Rom 8:11). Second, with regard to God the Son, Christ was sent "in order that the law's requirement would be fulfilled" (v. 4). The Son's work on the cross created an interchange whereby his righteousness through obedience is made available to humanity. "You are concerned to obtain acquittal from God. You cannot obtain it by your own efforts. God offers it to you freely through Jesus Christ."[10] However, forensic justification is not the entire description of the triune work of salvation. There is also the Spirit's work of creating our union with God. So, third, God the Holy Spirit "gives life because of righteousness" (v. 10). The Spirit of God takes the divine righteousness, which was commanded by the Father and fulfilled by the Son, and applies it to the believer.

While Paul elsewhere teaches of the Father's role and of the Son's role, the Holy Spirit's role in empowering and continuing the life of the Christian comes to the fore in this first section of Romans 8. The Spirit's work in maintaining the life of the Christian after its creation is manifested through various contrasts. The Christian will "walk," a term indicating long-term ethical conduct, "according to

---

[10] Kirk, *The Epistle to the Romans*, 56.

the Spirit" rather than "according to the flesh" (v. 4). The Christian will likewise "live according to the Spirit" rather than "according to the flesh" (v. 5). Finally, the Christian will have "the mind-set of the Spirit [in] life and peace" rather than "the mind-set of the flesh," which ends in "death" (v. 6).

The Indwellings of God. The Holy Spirit's manifest work in human life is the result of God sovereignly and continually uniting Godself with human beings.[11] In Romans 8, the indwelling of God with believers is put in distinctly trinitarian terms. And the Holy Spirit is, at least in part, the personal locus of that triune indwelling. With regard to the first person of the Trinity, the Holy Spirit is the Spirit "of God" and the Spirit "of him who raised Jesus from the dead" (vv. 9, 11). With regard to the second person of the Trinity, the Holy Spirit is the Spirit "of Christ" (v. 9). While Paul elsewhere in his corpus puts primary emphasis upon being "in Christ," in Romans 8 he mentions the Son (and the Father) but focuses on life with regard to the third person of the Trinity, that is, "in the Spirit" (v. 9).

Notice the two distinct forms of mutuality in Paul's description of union with God. First, there is the mutual indwelling of the Spirit with Christ and God—*God is with God.* Second, there is the mutuality of believers existing in God, or of God existing in believers—*God is with believing humanity.* The first indwelling is by nature, God with God; the second indwelling is by grace, God with the believer. The first indwelling, of God with God, is that while "Christ is in you" (v. 10), so also "the Spirit of God lives in you" (v. 9). Christ and the Spirit indwell each other even as the two indwell the believer. The second indwelling, of God with the believer, says

---

[11] Humanity here needs to be considered both individually and corporately. The plural, which could be taken either in a distributive or a corporate sense, is used several times in this passage (e.g. vv. 1, 5, 9a, 10a, 11, 13–15), even while the singular is also used (e.g., vv. 2, 9b, 10b).

that being "in the Spirit" is the same as knowing both that "Christ is in you" and that "the Spirit of God lives in you" (vv. 9–11). The three persons indwell one another in unity by nature, but the three persons indwell the believer in unity by grace.[12] The two different types of indwelling—by nature and by grace—must be kept distinct.

Also notice that the transcendent description of the believer being "in" God is balanced by the immanent description of God, through the Spirit and Christ, as being "in" the believer. The believers' existence "in" Christ and "in" the Spirit should not be seen as substantially different from Christ and the Spirit residing "in" believers. That said, the prior form, of believers existing in God, is the majority New Testament teaching. The number of times that the phrase "in Christ," is used far exceeds in number all of the occurrences of the "Christ in you" type of language. The believer's life with God is enabled by the cross of Jesus Christ and actuated by the uniting work of the Holy Spirit. Jesus Christ is identified as "the life" (John 14:6), but the Spirit is also identified as "life" (Rom 8:2). For believers to have life, they must thus be united with Christ by the Spirit, a unity that inundates the lives of believers.

Finally, note that although God as Spirit generates life within believers, believers do not exist as inanimate objects. They also have an active role, though it is definitively receptive rather than creative. The apostle, therefore, requires believers to pursue actively the Spirit's sovereign work of sanctification within themselves: "But if by the Spirit you put to death the deeds of the body, you will live" (v. 13). After this discussion regarding the believers' responsibility to

---

[12] In dogmatic terms, the eternal relations of mutual indwelling between the persons of the Godhead are known by the term *perichoresis*, or *interpenetration*, while the saving relation of the indwelling of God with believers is known by the terms *union* and *participation*.

follow the Spirit, Paul transitions to a discourse on the Spirit's role in beginning, maintaining, and consummating the Christian life.

The Spirit of Adoption

"For all those led by God's Spirit are God's sons" (v. 14). The next twelve verses in Romans 8 center around the Spirit's work of adoption in bringing many sons to God's glory (cf. John 1:12; Heb 2:10). In Roman society, there were two large primary social classes: those born into slavery and those born, adopted, or purchased into freedom. The life of slaves, who were substantial in number, was characterized economically by hard work and essentially by lack of personhood.[13] On the other side, those who were adopted received all the rights and substantial privileges of the natural sons of the *paterfamilias*. Paul used the Roman legal category of adoption to teach that there are, spiritually, two types of human beings. There are those who still exist in slavery to Satan, sin, and death. And then there are those who have been adopted out of slavery into divine sonship. God the Trinity adopts humans into a life of familial intimacy with God.

The temporal progress of adoption in the second section of Romans 8 enlightens our understanding of the beginning, continuance, and end of salvation by the Holy Spirit. First, the Father sent the Son to unite with our humanity, to atone for our sin, and to arise for our justification (Rom 4:25). The Son, however, does not work alone, for the Father also sends the Spirit to unite us with the Son. While we once were bound by a "spirit of slavery" to fear, we have since "received the Spirit of adoption" (8:15). Second, the Father and the

---

[13] Eduard Lohse, *The New Testament Environment*, trans. John E. Steely (Nashville: Abingdon, 1976), 212–14.

Son sent the Holy Spirit to testify these truths to our spirits and thence lead us to come before God as adopted sons. By the Spirit, we are able, with Christ to "cry out, 'Abba, Father'" (v. 16). The diminutive term *Abba* was commonly used in Palestinian households to indicate the intimate father–child relationship. It was not used of God by the Jews, but Jesus appropriated it so as to indicate that he was giving his disciples "a share in His relationship to God" (Mark 14:36; Gal 4:6).[14]

Third, having been adopted into a saving relation of sonship through faith by the Holy Spirit, we may now approach the Father with the testimony that we are also coheirs with the Son. The testimony to familial sonship and propertied heirship is made together between God's Spirit and our spirits (Rom 8:16–17). Finally, with regard to the consummation, Christians are reminded that they currently possess the Spirit as the "firstfruits" of the eventual harvest of their bodies to the resurrection life. "Adoption" is hereby defined eschatologically by Paul as "the redemption of our bodies" (v. 23).

Verses 14–25 trace the movement of spiritual adoption from its conception through its continuation to its consummation in the bodily resurrection. To speak of the "Spirit of adoption" functions as another way to describe the life-giving work of the Holy Spirit in uniting us with God as Trinity. The use of the connecting prefix *sym* or *syn*, "with" or "together with," further reinforces the union of the believer with God through the activity of the Spirit: The Holy Spirit "himself testifies together with our spirit" (*symmartyreo*; v. 16). Christian believers are "coheirs with Christ" (*sygkleronomoi*; v. 17). We are called to "suffer with" Christ (*sympascho*; v. 17) so that we might also "be glorified with him" (*syndoxazo*; v. 17). Against today's prevailing Western Christian ethos, we must remember that

---

[14] Cranfield, *The Epistle to the Romans*, 1:399–400.

suffering with Christ precedes glory with Christ. The Holy Spirit unites the Christian with Christ so that he or she participates in the whole life and death and resurrection of our sovereign Lord and passionate Savior. To an even more personal description of that union by the apostle we now turn our attention.

The Spirit of Intercession

Paul habitually and compellingly integrates not only his theological concerns but his linguistic method of conveying those ideas. While the subject of adoption extends throughout Rom 8:14–25, there is no hard shift after verse 25. Rather, the subject matter of verse 26 brings to its pinnacle a set of themes that first cropped up in verse 18. The Spirit of intercession (vv. 26–27) is required because of the "sufferings of this present time" (v. 18). The sufferings of the present are only bearable due to the "hope" (vv. 24–25) of the "glory that is going to be revealed" (v. 18). Verses 19–22 discuss how the rest of creation was subjected to decay. Creation now groans for the redemption that will come with "the glorious freedom of God's children" (v. 21). Verse 23 then transitions from the groaning of creation to the groaning of the people of God as they await "the redemption of our bodies."

How can human beings, who suffer under the trauma of sin's effects on creation and on the human body, find hope? Christ Jesus unquestionably died for our sins and arose for our justification. But how do we personally appropriate the hope that comes with Christ's atonement for us and justification of us? This is the work of the Holy Spirit. But why do we require the Holy Spirit's initiative on our behalf? The answer begins with the problem of our depravity, which Paul's discussion in Rom 1:18–3:23 demonstrated at length.

The human being does not even understand what the problem entails, never mind what the solution is.

The problem includes both our lack of knowledge and our lack of desire: "There is no one who understands; there is no one who seeks God" (3:11). The solution to humanity's predicament is not understood by man, nor is it desired by man. "There is no fear of God before their eyes" (v. 18). We do not pray correctly to God for our salvation because we do not understand the true severity of the problem we have. Karl Barth summarized the handicap we all suffer well: "Our mind is never right."[15] This is why Paul elsewhere stated that he dares not judge himself, much less allow any other human being to make spiritual judgments about him (1 Cor 3:4): Humans possess neither the mind nor the will to judge themselves, so we also lack the ability even to request of God what we really require.

Romans 8:26 informs us that our radical inability and spiritual blindness, both of which naturally lead us to despair, are why the Holy Spirit must work on our behalf. "In the same way the Spirit also helps us in our weakness, because we do not know what to pray for as we should, but the Spirit himself intercedes for us with unspoken groanings." Certain scholars, such as Ernst Käsemann, have argued that the critical issue Paul is considering here is the worship phenomenon of glossolalia. However, Cranfield is convinced that the problem concerns something more foundational, something soteriological.[16] Moo agrees: "The wording of the clause indicates that it is not the manner, or style, of prayer that Paul has in view but the content, or object, of prayer—what we are to pray for."[17]

---

[15] Karl Barth, *The Epistle to the Romans*, 6th ed., trans. Edwyn C. Hoskyns (New York: Oxford University Press, 1933), 317.

[16] Cranfield, *The Epistle to the Romans*, 1:422–23.

[17] Moo, *The Epistle to the Romans*, 523.

There are several reasons to deem Cranfield and Moo correct here. First, Romans 8 as a whole considers personal salvation as the culmination of the argument that has been emerging since chapter 1. The problem of speaking in tongues does not arise until the pragmatic issues have begun to be considered in chapter 12. And while Paul lists various spiritual gifts in that later chapter, speaking in tongues is not one of them (12:3–9). That particular issue is a major concern in Paul's Corinthian correspondence, but not in his letter to the Romans. Second, glossolalia has to do with praises, while the "groanings" concern Christian needs. Third, the term *alaletois*, which could be translated as "unspoken" or even "ineffable," literally means "without speaking." An audible oral phenomenon is being considered, if at all, only in its absence, not in its practice. The Spirit comes upon the human being to assist her where she cannot even begin to form the words of petition to God that are required.

The verb for "intercedes" here is of a highly unusual construction. Indeed, the term is not found in Greek outside of the New Testament and later Christian literature.[18] The verb *entygchano* sufficiently conveys the idea of intercession and is used in Rom 8:27. However, in verse 26, the prefix *hyper* is affixed to the same verb. *Hyperentygchano* could be translated simply as "intercede," or more literally as "intercede beyond." The Holy Spirit helps us by interceding for us in a way that is definitely beyond our capability. Our capacity for prayer has been corrupted by sin, and the Holy Spirit of God superintends our prayers so that sin no longer may continue to inhibit either our knowledge or our desire.

Verse 27 firmly grounds the work of the Holy Spirit as Intercessor in the trinitarian economy of salvation: "And he who searches our hearts knows the mind of the Spirit, because he intercedes

---

[18] Cranfield, *The Epistle to the Romans*, 1:423.

for the saints according to the will of God." The Spirit takes the lead in intercession, but the Son and the Father are also active. First, notice that the Spirit acts in two places simultaneously. The Spirit intercedes in the human heart "with unspoken groanings" (v. 26). At the same time, the Spirit is resident in heaven with God. Second, notice that it is the Son in heaven "who searches our hearts" by means of the Spirit (v. 27). Paul alluded to 1 Sam 16:7, where, as we explained in chapter 2, "the LORD sees the heart." The "Lord" is explicitly equated with Christ the Son elsewhere in Paul's writings (1 Cor 8:6), so Paul likely implied the Son here. Adding weight to this argument is that later in Romans 8, the intercessory work of the Son is located with him in heaven: "Christ Jesus is the one who died, but even more, has been raised; he also is at the right hand of God and intercedes for us" (v. 34). Third, it is "according to the will of God," the Father, that the Son intercedes through "the mind of the Spirit" (v. 27). Paul thereby concludes the third section of Romans 8 with a thick trinitarian description of the work of the Holy Spirit in the salvation of the human being.

Summary

Who is the Holy Spirit to believers? In Rom 8:1–13, the apostle described him as the Spirit of life, who brings salvation to believers. In verses 14–25, Paul defined him as the Spirit of adoption, for he unites the believer in a familial relation to Christ with God. Finally, in verses 26 and 27, Paul identified the Holy Spirit as the Intercessor, for only he can do in the human heart the work required for communion with God. In these ways, Paul repeatedly grounded the person of the Spirit in the triune life and the work of the Spirit in the triune economy. He shows how God indwells the believer through the initiating, sustaining, and consummating work of the Holy Spirit. Paul portrays the person of the Holy Spirit as the sovereign God through the way the Spirit works salvation into our persons.

The power of Romans 8 is not found merely in its trustworthy propositions about God the Spirit but also in its compelling description of the believer's transforming encounter with God through the personal work of the Holy Spirit. The Holy Spirit graciously comes from God the Father and from Christ Jesus to bring us the life we do not deserve. That God would take such an interest in us sinners and personally come, both as Son and as Holy Spirit, to restore communion with him ought to fill us with thanksgiving. That the Holy Spirit would personally indwell us and unite us with the Son and with the Father ought to drive us to worship God. The Holy Spirit takes us out of our fallen state and places us in the family of God. We become by grace God's children through the Spirit's personal application to us of the electing will of the Father, performed in the atoning work of Christ. The Holy Spirit, moreover, intercedes for us, simply because we have no capability whatsoever to intercede for ourselves. We originally don't even know how to verbalize what we need so that we might properly pray for salvation. The Spirit graciously does for us in salvation, from its conception through its continuation to its completion, what we cannot do for ourselves. Such profound knowledge of the Spirit's personal grace ought to compel us to worship God as the Father, as the Son, and, yes, also as the Holy Spirit.

CONCLUSION

Who Is the Holy Spirit to You?

Then he showed me the river of the water of life, clear as crystal, flowing from the throne of God and of the Lamb down the middle of the city's main street. The tree of life was on each side of the river, bearing twelve kinds of fruit, producing its fruit every month. The leaves of the tree are for healing the nations, and there will no longer be any curse. The throne of God and of the Lamb will be in the city, and his servants will worship him. (Rev 22:1–3)

S cripture both begins and ends with a garden scene. At the end of Scripture, the garden is watered by a very special river. This river of "the water of life" flows from "the throne of God and of the Lamb." It runs through a city, the New Jerusalem, supplying life forever to God's people gathered there. We have already seen how the canon of Scripture affiliates the Spirit with both "water" and "life." At the revelation of the *Eschaton*, the person who brings "the water of life" proceeds from the throne where two other persons reign. As detailed in chapter 5, John's Gospel describes the Spirit as the One who gives life through being sent into the hearts of people from both the Father and the Son. Similarly, John's Apocalypse pictures eternal life as moving in the Holy Spirit toward redeemed humanity from "God" and "the Lamb." This promise of the gift of an eternal life experienced with God the Trinity is the beatific vision for which our hearts hope.

This book was written to answer the general question, Who is the Holy Spirit? In seeking that answer, three major pneumatological texts from the Old Testament and three from the New Testament were explored in depth. More particularly, we have been asking, "What have these exercises in the theological interpretation of Scripture revealed about the Holy Spirit?" We will not here endeavor to recount all our discoveries. The "Summary" paragraphs at the end of each chapter are intended to help anyone seeking that level of detail. Instead, now I will offer a more holistic or philosophical worship-oriented review to answer an existential query: "Who is the Holy Spirit to you?"

Two ways of thinking about the identity of the Spirit, one negative and one positive, need to be considered in formulating a response to such a difficult question. By "negative theology," we do not mean that there is something critical to say against the Holy Spirit. Rather, we mean that there are certain things that we cannot say about the Holy Spirit, because he is beyond us and has not revealed all things regarding himself. Contrariwise, by "positive theology," we mean that there are things we definitely can and should say about the Holy Spirit due to divine revelation. We may not say some things about the Spirit of God due to his transcendence, even as there are some things we should say about the Spirit of God due to his self-revelation. We will begin with negative theology, proceed to positive theology, and conclude with a call to worship.

Negative Theology

The first thing that must be said about the identity of the Holy Spirit concerns what has *not* been revealed. As we discovered in chapter 1, there was nothing other than God, the Spirit of God, and the Word of God at the beginning. The Holy Spirit thus cannot, by reason of his preexistence, be captured by reference to created things. As Karl Barth noted, the Holy Spirit is God and, therefore, beyond human definition. "We know Him to be actus purus, pure reality and occurrence, unlimited and unconfined, without beginning or end, place or time. We know Him to be no thing among other things, not even a thing at all, not even the supreme thing."[1]

Barth is not saying that the Spirit of God lacks reality. Quite the opposite! The famous Swiss theologian is saying that the Spirit as ultimate reality exceeds our natural ability to know him. The Holy Spirit, because he is God, is transcendent, so far above us that there can be no knowledge of him apart from the divine grace of revelation. And this revelation, because God accommodates himself to use human words, occurs only by analogy between the Creator and his creature. Again, the Spirit is God, so he must remain mysterious. We know of him only by the gift of revelation, and we know of his character only by analogous comparison to the things he created out of nothing.

The transcendent mystery of the Spirit is intended to drive us toward worship of the Spirit. We cannot grasp the Holy Spirit, but he can grasp us by grace. The Spirit's radical independence and our utter dependence on him compel us to worship him as the God far above and effectively beyond humanity, the God who nonetheless condescends to come to us in love. "Who is the Holy Spirit?" "The

---

[1] Barth, *The Epistle to the Romans*, 274 (see chap. 6, n. 15).

question contains in itself the answer, namely, that the Spirit—IS."[2] This is the most positive thing that a theology of mystery, a negative theology, may say about God the Spirit.

Positive Theology

The second thing we can affirm about the Spirit's identity is that, in spite of his mysteriousness and our ignorance, a great deal must still be said about God the Holy Spirit. We should speak about the Holy Spirit's identity because of his self-revelation in the Word of God. There is a paradox here. The mystery of God drives us to speechless worship, but the revelation of God drives us to speak toward a worship full of words. Paul, as explained in chapter 6, understood that we are incapable of truly knowing and worshiping God unless he performs a miracle in our hearts. And that miracle must begin with the election of God the Father, must center in the atonement and resurrection of God the Son, and must culminate with the personal intercession of God the Holy Spirit. This type of knowing worship drives us to use a great many words, words of praise about who God is, as Father, as Son, and as Holy Spirit.

All six of the previous chapters, therefore, contain positive descriptions of the Holy Spirit. Yes, the Spirit is mysterious, but he is also the mighty Mover (ch. 1). The Spirit reveals himself as the sovereign Lord God (ch. 2). Scripture repeatedly identifies the Spirit in an explicitly trinitarian manner. The Spirit proceeds eternally from God the Father and possesses the fullness of the Godhead and all of the divine perfections along with the Father and the Son (ch. 5). He conceived Jesus, commissioned Jesus to his threefold Christological

---

[2] Barth, 272.

office, and accompanied Jesus through his ministry, death, and resurrection (ch. 4).

Scripture identifies the relationship of the Spirit to creation in such a way that the Spirit remains simultaneously transcendent and immanent. He sovereignly convicts the world of its sin of unbelief in God, of the righteousness of Jesus Christ, and of the coming judgment (ch. 5). The Holy Spirit's intercession brings the repentant believer to confess the perfections of God, to confess his sinfulness against God, and to petition for a restoration of fellowship for the purpose of worship (ch. 3). He comes to indwell personally the believing disciple of Jesus Christ, bringing her forever into communion with the triune life through filial adoption and intimate intercession (ch. 6).

Paradox and Worship

So, yes, there is much positive that we can and must speak about the Holy Spirit, even as we should exercise prudence in not saying too much. Karl Barth concurs with this judgment: we "must, paradoxically, worship Him as the third Person of the Godhead, await Him, pray for Him, and, confident in His peculiar and particular and quite definite action, be silent in the presence of His power and take care lest we should cause Him tribulation."[3] The theology of the Holy Spirit, because it is about God, the unknown God who makes himself known in revelation, necessitates a dialectical exercise in negative theology and in positive theology.

"Who is the Holy Spirit to you?" Providing the answer requires extreme care. On the one hand, we must remain silent when it comes to trying to enclose the Holy Spirit in some merely human definition.

---

[3] Barth, 274.

After all, "He is completely the Other."[4] On the other hand, we must also speak of him. We must speak of him because he is the God who reveals himself in order to remove our sinful ignorance. We must speak of him because he is the God who created us. We must speak of him because he is the God who applies to us the redemption wrought by Jesus. We must speak of him because he is the God who will bring all things to their final end. We must speak of him with words of praise, because the Bible hereby indicates that he is a person and that he is divine.

We must also hear the Spirit speak to us personally. From the end of all things, the Holy Spirit, along with the Father and the Lamb, calls out to all of humanity in the here and now to believe the gospel with his church.

> Both the Spirit and the bride say, "Come!" Let anyone who hears, say, "Come!" Let the one who is thirsty come. Let the one who desires take the water of life freely. (Rev 22:17)

Reader, what about you? Will you embrace true life even now? Do you hear the electing voice of the Father speaking the good news that he has given his only begotten Son to die for your sins and to arise from the dead for your life? Do you hear the Son speaking the words of the Father, revealing his love for you in his death and resurrection? Do you hear the Holy Spirit speaking across time and space to you, *"Come and freely drink this water of eternal life"*? The Spirit is the source of the water that can spring up to eternal life within you. If you believe in the gospel of Jesus Christ through the sovereign work of the Spirit, then come with me and let us together

---

4 Barth, 275.

worship God the Father, God the Son, and, yes, also God the Holy Spirit, for the Spirit, too, is the eternal God. Reader, who is the Holy Spirit to you?

Further Suggested Resources

Cole, Graham A. *He Who Gives Life: The Doctrine of the Holy Spir-it.* Wheaton, IL: Crossway, 2007.

Congar, Yves. *I Believe in the Holy Spirit*, translated by Gary Chap-man, 3 volumes in 1. New York: Crossroad Herder, 1997.

Fee, Gordon D. *God's Empowering Presence: The Holy Spirit in the Letters of Paul.* Reprint, Grand Rapids: Baker Academic, 2009.

Levering, Matthew. *Engaging the Doctrine of the Holy Spirit: Love and Gift in the Trinity and the Church.* Grand Rapids: Baker Academic, 2016.

Swete, Henry Barclay. *Holy Spirit in the New Testament: A Study of Primitive Christian Teaching.* London: Macmillan, 1910.

Thiselton, Anthony C. *The Holy Spirit: In Biblical Teaching, through the Centuries, and Today.* Grand Rapids: Eerdmans, 2013.

Yarnell, Malcolm B., III. "The Doctrine of the Holy Spirit: The Per-son and Work of the Holy Spirit," in *A Theology for the Church*, edited by Daniel L. Akin. Rev. ed. Nashville: B&H Academic, 2014.

———. *God the Trinity: Biblical Portraits.* Nashville: B&H Aca-demic, 2016.

Name and Subject Index

Scripture Index

131

Scripture Index